THE SCIENCE OF
SPIRITUAL MARKETING

INITIATION INTO MAGNETISM

More Praise . . .

"In today's world, business owners and marketers are faced with ethical and moral marketing choices that are vitally important for the welfare of our entire culture and the earth as a whole. One marketing path leads to rampant consumerism and blind, unsustainable materialism; another leads to wise choices that honor the earth, our climate, and the fate of future generations.

"In *The Science of Spiritual Marketing: Initiation into Magnetism*, Andrea Adler sensitizes people in all professions to these issues and enables them to choose wisely. It is crucial that her message be heard."

Larry Dossey, MD, author of
The Extraordinary Healing Power of Ordinary Things and *Healing Words*

"Andrea Adler's new book, *The Science of Spiritual Marketing*, turns the normal marketing paradigm on its head and proposes a new business equation that should be taught in all business schools: an authentic story + a product or service that benefits mankind = a magnet for success."

Miriam Knight, CEO, *New Consciousness Review*

"As our business culture evolves from Capitalism 1.0, where self-interest trumps community interest, to Capitalism 2.0, where self-interest and community interest are sustainably integrated, it needs to develop a new, more authentic voice. *The Science of Spiritual Marketing* is a roadmap for navigating this evolutionary journey."

Joseph McCormick, cofounder, Reuniting America

"For the first time, an author has captured the true essence of marketing. It is a soul method. Marketing is about spirit, and Andrea introduces the methodology brilliantly."

Joia Jefferson Nuri, President
In the Public Eye Communications

"Adler sets a new high-water mark! A book every business strategist, CEO, owner, or marketing consultant will want to read . . . and read again. Clearly lays a pathway for the visionary or hands-on manager seeking to grow their business."

Martin Rosenberg, PhD, Chairman
Santa Fe Film Festival

"Andrea's paradigm signals the beginning of a great new direction in honest, direct communication between marketing clients and their audience. Learning about the history of the perceived 'evils' of marketing gives one the knowledge and confidence necessary to move forward with a clean conscience, renewed vigor, and—let's face it—newfound joy.

"Thank you, Andrea. I feel better already! Integrating what's important to me makes me feel so much better about shouting my own praises from the rooftops."

Jim Tomlinson, The Sage Post, Jerome, AZ

"Hard-core business types will be pleasantly surprised at how this book hits home. Andrea's holistic approach is just what Madison Avenue needs to get their message through to today's jaded consumers who have learned to tune out much of our marketing messages.

"This lady transcends the gulf between the business world and what we used to call 'Eastern thinking.' Go into this book with an open mind and be rewarded beyond your expectations."

Kenneth E. Guard, Certified Financial Planner, Fort Myers, FL

"If you want to live a life with new consciousness, personally and professionally, *The Science of Spiritual Marketing: Initiation into Magnetism* must become your bible; otherwise you will be pouring your wisdom into old paradigm models of business and marketing that are dead and dying.

"You owe it to yourself and the world to hitch your dream to the brightest star of movement. Andrea Adler opens the gate! If you are ready for magic in your world, read this book!"

Kay Snow-Davis, President, Global Family Education Center, Inc.

THE SCIENCE OF SPIRITUAL MARKETING

INITIATION INTO MAGNETISM

ANDREA ADLER

Prasad Publishing

Santa Fe, New Mexico

505-983-7777

Prasad Publishing
PO Box 31637
Santa Fe, New Mexico 87594

Permissions will be found with the Notes.

Cover design by Desert Elements,
www.desertelements.com

Text, typography, and book design by Denton Lesslie,
www.dentonsdesigns.com

Library of Congress Cataloging-in-Publication Data available upon request.

First printing, October 2007
ISBN-10-09715243-4-3
ISBN-13-978-0-9715243-4-7

andrea@HolisticPR.com
www.HolisticPR.com
505-983-7777

Dedicated to the Siddhas,
and to Brian, Damo, and Sarah.

CONTENTS

THE JOURNEY OF INITIATION   i

Chapter 1
THE ROOT CHAKRA OF PR   1

Chapter 2
CONNECTING TO SOURCE   13

Chapter 3
ALIGNING WITH OUR SOUL'S CALLING   25

Chapter 4
THE THREE STAGES OF CREATIVITY   37

Chapter 5
MOVING BEYOND OUR COMFORT ZONES   51

Chapter 6
THE POWER OF OUR STORY   61

Chapter 7
RITUAL AND CEREMONY   77

Chapter 8
MIND MAPPING   89

Chapter 9
OUR SOULFUL COLLATERAL   101

Chapter 10
BUILDING BRIDGES   117

Chapter 11
Leveraging Our Assets   133

Chapter 12
Responding from Abundance: Sharing the Wealth   147

Chapter 13
Write to Learn   161

Chapter 14
The Element of Surprise   175

Chapter 15
Discipline   189

The Invitation to Embark   203

Thank-yous   207

Suggested Reading   211

Notes and Permissions   213

About the Author   221

THE JOURNEY OF INITIATION

Marketing is not only an art and a science; it is a divine practice, a synthesis of interconnected ideas that work in unison with the visible and the invisible, manifesting a profound alchemy.

Before any marketing materials, before any marketing strategies, there is a journey to be taken inside ourselves first. It is our connection to *source*—the indefinable place where all thoughts and actions arise and subside, where pure intelligence reveals itself and bestows upon us wisdom and light.

And then as Rumi, the Sufi poet, said, "There's a push and another push, the necessary dyings, the ground crumbling that lets wildflowers come up." [1]

The initiation into the Science of Spiritual Marketing is not unlike other initiations, where there is a quality of being that takes precedence and a universal plea that invites us to become the student again, where we adopt "beginner's mind."

When an artist steps up to a new canvas, there is a sense of awe, inspiration, and humility.

When a composer begins a new piece, there is a quality of vulnerability, an openness, to his or her listening.

To be in the true spirit of initiation, we graciously drop our ego, shed the familiar, and enter a doorway through which reinvention can take place.

Once we have taken this step, we find there are blocks to be removed, changes that need to take place so that openings for new possibilities can occur.

How we remain open to these changes is an individual undertaking, to be explored at our own time and at our own pace. These changes can be learned either from a living teacher or through our own personal experiences.

How we become initiated into the perpetual magnetism that draws us deep into the well of good fortune is a mystery I have observed for the past thirty years.

I have witnessed failures and successes.

I have seen lack of focus, the neediness of greed, and the willfulness of ego.

I've seen generous hearts, the desire to change, and tremendous leaps of faith.

It has been a fascinating journey, witnessing the decisions we make as we move through these stages of development.

We can be stopped by lack of insight and skillful means; or we can allow ourselves to be supported by the *chi*, the energy that can transform us.

By imbibing the spiritual and holistic concepts introduced in this book, we can manifest this chi more readily. We can create an outreach that resonates with who we are, without compromise. We can blossom as whole, integrated beings and enter into a world of infinite possibilities we never knew existed.

There are many aspects to this spiritual marketing. But the most impressive quality is how it transforms us energetically.

We begin to walk with a different rhythm.

Vibrate at a new frequency.

Speak from a place of conviction.

Move from fear to fearlessness.

From apprehension to one-pointedness.

From rigidity to fluidity.

From ignorance to higher wisdom.

And all along the way, we are reminded of Rumi's words: "There's a push and another push, the necessary dyings, the ground crumbling that lets wildflowers come up."

The initiation revealed in these chapters will not only drive you deeper into your true nature; it will expand your relationship to your own creativity, your business, and the many marketing concepts available to you. It is not intended to teach you how to compete, but how to think.

This initiation begins with you and your commitment to allow the wildflower to push through.

I invite you to partake in this enchanting journey of discovery with me.

Andrea Adler

CHAPTER 1

THE ROOT CHAKRA OF PR

Effective communication is 20 percent
what you know and 80 percent how
you feel about what you know.

— Jim Rohn, American businessman

Have you ever wondered why the words *public relations* and *marketing* have acquired such a harsh reputation? Why are people, especially those in creative fields, turned off by the mere mention of these words? Why are business owners so apprehensive to embark on a promotional campaign that could bring them the abundance and recognition they are yearning for?

I will attempt to address these questions, and provide answers and solutions—not only because of my own personal interest in this magical, mysterious process, but because I believe there are conscious and sensible ways to use public relations and marketing to grow our businesses, particularly when we approach them from a spiritual or holistic mindset.

Before I begin, however, I'd like to clarify the meaning of a few words and their relationship to this book. When the word *spiritual* is used, I do not mean "religious" or religion in any way. *Spiritual*, in the context of this book, has to do with an internal awareness, a sacred connection to oneself and one's work, a bond with the soul and the spirit that includes our relationship to ourselves and to the world. In the truest sense, spirituality is not "for" anything—not for marketing success, prosperity, good health, or fulfilling relationships. It is its own reward, as a consequence of connecting with *source*, wherever that source, that place of truth, exists within us. It also includes a conscious awareness, our moral compass regarding the products and services we offer—a compass without which the very concept of "spiritual marketing" becomes an oxymoron. Every contribution, every decision we make is so integrally connected with "the market"—consumption, lifestyle, manufacturing, buying, selling—that it's naturally connected with marketing and PR.

This spiritual dimension of our outreach requires that we look not only at *how* we are promoting our business, but *what* we are promoting. This is where we probe our souls, question our intentions, explore the moral fiber in our approach toward our clients, the planet, and ourselves.

When I speak of *holistic marketing*, I'm talking about an integrated, multidimensional approach that doesn't focus solely on the bottom line, but rather operates by synthesizing the whole picture. The key word here is *wholeness*. The wholeness of our intention, our message, our story, how we share our story, how other people share our story, and their feelings toward it. The wholeness of the person administering the business—and the wholeness of what we offer those we serve—will define our success.

Spiritual marketing is a *science* in the sense that it provides a rational understanding of an emerging worldview: the reuniting of science and spirituality. Science is a system of acquiring and organizing knowledge that reveals information about reality. In the same way, this book attempts to share reliable, concrete predictions about the science of spiritual marketing, gained through my research.

So, let us begin.

Too Much Noise

From the moment we are born and alert enough to perceive information on any level, we are inundated with advertisements that promote some product or service. Our senses are flooded by blaring hype, propaganda, political spin, and advertising that scream at us from the radio, TV, newspapers, billboards, telemarketers—and now from the Internet.

Advertisements are showing up in elevators and at the gas pump. They jingle and jangle before us on TV and in grocery-store checkout lanes. They have even made an appearance in restroom stalls and over public urinals. After trying countless ways to tune out the noise, customarily without victory, our brains have become so saturated, so numb, that the thought of using any of these venues to promote ourselves has become, to say the least, unattractive.

It's a shame to think we must turn away from the channels of communication that bring us pleasure in our leisure and benefit to our work in order to escape this overkill. This problem has been, in fact, the catalyst for me to initiate my search for a holistic/spiritual approach. By delving into the base *chakra*, the root cause and true nature, of PR itself, perhaps we can understand how this dilemma came to be, and how we can move out of it.

In the Beginning . . . There Was the Word

The "word of mouth." The undeniable outpouring of expression that stimulates us to take notice, and buy into a myriad of products or services. This natural, spontaneous "technique" of *word of mouth* began, I suspect, as early as the days of the Neanderthal—possibly even before. I can only imagine that when the first cave person developed a stone tool that could shape hand axes or scrape deerskins in half the time, he or she ran around gesticulating how the new instrument could do the job better, faster, easier. It didn't take long for the invention to spread to other cave dwellers. Soon, cave dwellers everywhere were developing similar tools of their own.

America is, after all, the land of word of mouth. Word of mouth brought our forebears to this new world. Word of mouth populated the first sparse settlements on the eastern shore, and then drew everyone westward. Word of mouth settled the frontier. In the late nineteenth century, as industries and cities grew, word spread to the farms and rural towns that jobs were available and that fortunes could be made by moving to the big cities. As a result, thousands of families moved away from their country settings hoping to improve their families' future. There were no TV or radio announcements made to inform these farmers about this opportunity. Still, the news spread.

Historically, word of mouth was, and still is, a powerful way to disseminate information. It is that face-to-face relationship with someone you know that establishes authenticity and credibility. Of course, if the object of the buzz is not authentic or doesn't live up to its expectation, the buzz will quickly die and bad press will take its place.

I am not proposing that word of mouth is the only way to create an outreach, or that advertising through traditional media can't be effective. I am purely sharing some thoughts about the word-of-mouth phenomenon. Both *The Tipping Point* by Malcolm Gladwell and *The Anatomy of Buzz* by Emanuel Rosen are books that extrapolate the word-of-mouth trend in greater detail and are, without question, books I highly recommend you add to your marketing library. We'll take a more detailed look at how to enhance our use of "word of mouth" in Chapter 10, Building Bridges.

So, how did we move from this simple, uncomplicated form of marketing to the media explosion and misuse we currently endure?

Media Propaganda

It is clear that a quantum shift, a watershed of demarcation, took place in how the media was used—manipulated, if you will—in 1924 during the administration of President Coolidge.

During this era, radios and automobiles emerged as the top-selling consumer products. For the first time, advertisers were able to mass-market their products, and the public had the resources to purchase them.

The widespread prosperity that followed World War I had catapulted the nation into a mass consumer economy, and President Coolidge set out to capitalize on the innovations. After an arduous search, he found and hired just the man to help him accomplish his new agenda: Edward Bernays, regarded as the founder of the field of public relations.

It is interesting to note that Bernays was the nephew of Sigmund Freud (double indemnity, as it were: his mother was Freud's sister; his father was Freud's wife's brother). We can only imagine the psychological edge he must have had. Bernays would come to orchestrate elaborate advertising and consumer spectacles for his corporate clients: the Dodge Brothers, Procter & Gamble, the American Tobacco Company, the General Electric Corporation, and many more.[1]

For instance, while working for the American Tobacco Company, Bernays mastered the link between corporate sales campaigns and popular social causes. He did this by persuading prominent women in New York City to hold up Lucky Strike cigarettes at a public event as symbolic "torches of freedom." Another clever global media affair Bernays originated was the "Light's Golden Jubilee," a worldwide celebration commemorating the fiftieth anniversary of the electric light bulb, sponsored (behind-the-scenes) by the General Electric Corporation.

Needless to say, his corporate sponsors thought Bernays was the best thing to come along since sliced bread. Word spread quickly and, as a result, Bernays became the first public-relations consultant to work on behalf of a United States president when he was hired to improve Coolidge's image for the 1924 presidential election.[2]

Out of concern that he was using advertising techniques to aid his political candidate, Bernays was accused of crossing the line between advertising and propaganda—in other words, selling the politician to voters as if Coolidge were toothpaste. Bernays defended his position and insisted that truth seeking and advertising need not be incompatible; he believed that the mass promotion of ideas was necessary to change society in beneficial directions.

And thus began the merchandising of politics in a whole new way.

The Marketing of Goods and Services

In the 1950s, television gained national popularity. Consumers could now *see* the products that they had previously only heard about. Corporations that could afford to advertise, did, and for the most part monopolized the commercial airwaves. Through aggressive and subliminal messages, advertisers directed millions of people toward the purchase of goods and services that, in the end, may not have led to their advancement or betterment.

Commercial advertising promoted cigarettes as a "cool" thing to do on a summer day; only later did we discover the deadly effects of nicotine and inhaled carcinogens. Milk manufacturers are still promoting dairy products as the best source of calcium for our bones, yet naturopathic and allopathic doctors alike are finding that dairy products do not necessarily "do the body good" and can trigger severe allergies. Research has documented the harmful effects diet drinks have on our teeth and organs—not to mention the cancer-causing and neurologically overstimulating sugar substitutes, saccharin and aspartame, used to sweeten these drinks. Fast food, household chemicals, and the pesticides we eat and breathe all contribute to climbing death rates. And don't even get me started on the overconsumption of pharmaceutical drugs and the detrimental side effects they create in the body, or the destructive products damaging our environment and our global atmosphere.

Not only are the above-mentioned products slowly but surely destroying our inner and outer environments, but the overload of information and sensory stimulation has contributed to many of the diseases prevalent on our planet today: obesity, diabetes, asthma, migraines, ADHD, and Alzheimer's. Particularly Alzheimer's! If you think about it, with the surfeit of messages we are subjected to, by the time we reach our seventies and eighties, dementia begins to look like the only way out.

The New Paradigm

There needs to be a shift. There needs to be a way to restore the integrity of marketing and public relations, as both a process and a profession. Not only for the consumer, but for the conscious business owner and the marketing consultant who wants to promote his or her clients ethically and become more conscious about the actual products and services being promoted.

Some years ago, I began to contemplate these issues . . . rather obsessively. I watched how people from various professions struggled with how to define themselves, how to reach their audiences in ways that were provocative and stimulating, while at the same time uplifting rather than degrading. How to create marketing strategies that were ethical and memorable. I would observe how businesses tried to stop manipulative actions and practice "truth in advertising," but would inevitably fall back and repeat approaches they disliked—because they didn't know any other way.

Then I had an overnight revelation that took thirty years to materialize. I realized that many business owners had not journeyed inside themselves first. They had not asked those pertinent questions that would bring them more into alignment with the spiritual aspect of their nature and of their business, but were, instead, "shooting from the hip."

I saw how thousands of dollars were being spent by earnest businesspeople to learn their respective fields, and yet, when it came time to open their business and start marketing it, they were in the dark. They had no idea how to start, let alone proceed. They would hire marketing consultants, but many of these consultants performed their job like allopathic doctors and mechanics, looking at only one part of the body, without considering the whole picture—the mental, emotional, social, and spiritual implications of the campaign. In addition, many of these consultants didn't care what their clients were promoting, even if it meant killing wildlife, polluting the environment, or destroying the planet.

For marketers in the new paradigm, integrity needs to be top on the list. Instead of jumping in with all fours for the monetary rewards, we must ask ourselves: Does this client resonate with who I am and the kind of business I want to represent? Are they missing the mark? And if so, how can I support them to reconnect with what is important? Our responsibility is to steward our clients, guide them to Oz—the future they want to experience—so they are aware of where their "Yellow Brick Road" starts and ends.

We walk a fine line when we start writing our clients' material. Our true role as marketers is to help clients access their vision, their innate wisdom, in a process that brings their deepest yearnings to the forefront—so that it's their words, their images that resonate with the audience they want to attract, not ours.

If more marketers would understand and use this process, people's faith in the profession would be renewed, the vital force of public relations would return, and business owners would be more apt to pursue positive, life-enhancing marketing options.

As entrepreneurs, sole proprietors, and CEOs, it is time to take responsibility for the products and services we are introducing. It's time to ask ourselves: How is my business serving me, and the gifts I have to offer? How is my business helping my audience, and the world at large? Because we are living during a critical moment in human and planetary history, when global warming, capitalism, and consumerism are at a heightened peak, these spiritual/holistic inquiries are more fundamental than ever.

THE RESURRECTION

I first introduced this holistic/spiritual approach to traditional business owners in New York in the early eighties. There was limited interest. Most of the immediate attention came from the complementary-therapy community, as they had a clear, well-developed understanding of energy and the energetic response words, feelings and, in this case, marketing, have on the whole body. They understood karma, the cause and effect associated with a product or service and the spiritual ramifications it would have, both overtly and subtly.

It was only after 9/11 that more businesses became interested in Holistic PR. It was only after our lives and our trust in the United States and all forms of "business as usual" had fallen apart, when our comfortable lifestyles were uprooted and our collective minds had shifted from seeing life in black and white to seeing variable shades of many colors, that previously unquestioned values were suddenly up for grabs. For many, there was an unparalleled opening to questioning, and reevaluation. The business owners who were coming to me for marketing knew they had to find other ways to reach their audience, and more personal, heartfelt ways to express themselves. They began to ask more meaningful questions: Are we stimulating fear in our audience? Are we being hypocritical? Are our products causing harm? Are we truly serving our audience and their best interest, and if so, by what means?

And all of us, as consumers, found ourselves looking for more substance and meaning in what we listened to, watched, and bought. This opening of the heart, this change in consciousness, forever altered not only the way we lived our lives, but the way marketing would be approached and received.

LESS FEAR—MORE LOVE

The dissemination of fear is something we have all experienced and even seen escalate in our lifetime. Whether it comes from a political machine, a terrorist cell, a pharmaceutical company, or the Weather Channel, fear has become the archetypal tactic. Fear cripples. It cripples our thoughts, our creativity, our freedom of choice, and our motivation. When a government, an organization, or a company uses this approach to market their products or ideologies, and we are unconscious of its effect, it neutralizes our senses, subliminally weakens the moral fiber of our being, and creates a culture of apathy, frailty, and anxiety.

Holistic marketing is the antithesis of this. We don't use fear tactics. We find ways to soothe the spirit and build trust through personal participation. We design messages that create ease, through truthfulness and an expanded, uplifting point of view, and therefore connect with our audience in stronger ways. By honoring the mind, body, and spirit as a unity, we create a climate in which our audience looks forward to our information rather than turning away from it. From the beginning of what we do to the very end, everything gets processed through our spiritual values and holistic view.

As business owners, entrepreneurs, and consultants, we can continue to pollute the planet and the media with superfluous images and text; or we can fill the hearts and minds of our audience with information that uplifts the planet and the spirit, and thereby creates a more beneficent result. We have the opportunity to design, manufacture, and promote products that have integrity in the marketplace. When our story is authentic and our product and service benefit mankind and live up to our promises, we can trust that word of mouth will spread the news with less effort than we can imagine.

When the context of our public-relations efforts is in alignment with our content and we understand that we have a moral and social purpose to uphold, when we understand that emotional connection is the true driving force and that we don't have to manipulate our content to get our audience's attention, then the words *public relations* and *marketing* will no longer be greeted with hesitation or negativity. Instead, operating from the spiritual/holistic concepts of wholeness and integration, our mindful outreach will be understood as a crucial part of making our offerings known, and people will feel inclined to explore the messages in the materials we create.

FOR FURTHER CONTEMPLATION

At the end of each chapter, a series of contemplations will be offered as an invitation to dive deeper into an experience of the material. These questions can be a vehicle for you to reflect on what you've just read, explore new approaches, catch sparks of inspiration, and brainstorm new possibilities and applications. As you begin the initiation process, you may want to journal your responses.

1. Has your understanding regarding PR and marketing changed while reading this chapter? If so, how?

2. Are the products and services you are promoting in alignment with your truth? Are they credible and beneficial to you, your clients, and the planet?

3. What are the ways and means you are using to attract your audience? Do you subliminally pressure your audience, or do you educate and inform them?

4. Are you in your truth and integrity with your message, both in its content and in the way you present it?

5. What would holistic marketing actually look like for you? For your business?

6. What aspects of holistic marketing might benefit your business and outreach?

7. What changes do you need to make to create a more spiritual or holistic approach?

CHAPTER 2

CONNECTING TO SOURCE

Set fire to the Self within by the practice of meditation. Be drunk with the wine of divine love. Thus shall you reach perfection.

— *Shvetashvatara Upanishad*

Whenever we take on the promise of becoming initiated into anything, there is an opening within, a letting go of what was, and a curiosity of what soon may be. The mere thought of initiation can bring up apprehension, concern for the unknown, and unease as to what the initiation may introduce. We can back away from this feeling of trepidation and not take any action . . . remaining where we are in our lives. Or we can move ahead—even if there is fear—and trust that when we take this leap into uncharted realms, a safety net will surely appear.

The ease of initiation manifests most gracefully when we are connected to *source:* that place inside us where consciousness resides, where we feel rooted, comfortable in our own skin, whether we are active or at rest. When we merge into this space, we have more trust in our decisions; we are able to work through emotional and physical challenges, and maintain objectivity. By surrendering into this relationship, by tending to this "inner garden" first, we move more quickly out of confusion and agitation; we act with increasing clarity.

Take a moment and think of the ways in which *you* connect with source. Perhaps it's when you're walking on the beach, mountain climbing, skiing, or swimming. Maybe it's when you are jogging or knitting. Isn't it true that while these activities nourish the soul and uplift the spirit, they require an attention to and a focus on something *outside* ourselves?

The act of meditation is quite different. It is a journey that takes us *inside* ourselves. It becomes the gateway through which we can dive into our psyche and perform self-inquiry. It is a practice that allows us to witness our senses and our emotions, building an internal muscle that strengthens the mind. It also reveals our limitations—and shows us our greatness.

There are numerous forms of meditation, from open-eyed to closed-eyed, from a simple mindfulness of the breath to a meditation that focuses on an image, on a subtle feeling, or on a mantra. There are Christian, Buddhist, Hindu, Taoist, Jewish, and Islamic forms of meditation. And while each of these methods has its own unique qualities, they all provide a respite from our everyday routines, allowing us to observe ourselves from an objective point of view—a kind of telescopic, microscopic vision into our internal mechanics. Whether we sit with eyes closed or open, this essential human experience offers us an opportunity like no other: to engage fully in the pursuit of looking inward.

MEDITATION IS THE FIRST STEP

I introduce meditation early on because it is the starting point for the rest of the journey to unfold. Whatever one's spiritual path or tradition, meditation is the fundamental technology for experiencing the depth of reality. For it is only when we have learned to quiet the mind, to surrender our thoughts and settle into stillness and to allow this stillness to expand, that we can begin to access our inner knowing. Only when we have heard the subtle voice of wisdom within, recognized it, and acted on it with faith and trust can we begin to understand Spirit and how it moves us.

How can there possibly be a successful marketing strategy, campaign, or initiative without listening to our inner guidance first? How many times have you heard yourself say, *Oh, I wish I had trusted my instincts and purchased that building,* or *I wish I had said yes and gone to that seminar,* or *No, don't you dare get involved with that project, it's toxic!* How often do we even hear that voice, let alone act on it? The more we practice meditation, the more audible that voice becomes, and the more capable we are of hearing it. This is the gift we receive when we sit for meditation.

I have met many people who think meditation is a waste of time, or who think it's boring. Active people, who would prefer to be "doing something." "Who has the time?" "Nothing's happening when I sit," they say. I always get a kick out of hearing that one. Particularly because my experience is that when I sit, even while I am still, I feel like I'm taking the posture of the hummingbird, that magnificent aerodynamic phenomenon able to hover in midair for hours. That tiny, jewel-feathered warrior may create the illusion of being suspended effortlessly, but the truth is, his wings are beating at a speed of up to 200 strokes per second.

That's what it's like when we meditate. Although we are just sitting, we are extremely active. When we begin to feel its true worth and power, there is an ongoing plunge into the depths of our soul. There we connect with insights and revelations about ourselves that we may never otherwise encounter. Internal shifts begin to occur, emotions are transmuted, and stagnant places get charged.

In other words, meditation is not for the weak or for the judgmental; it is only for lovers of wisdom. And those who are courageous enough to go there will certainly receive its wondrous fruits.

My Introduction to Meditation

Meditation has always been the tool I have used to unite myself with source. It's the one discipline that has provided me with, and been a catalyst for, peace and fearlessness. It has supported me through harrowing times and delightful times. In every situation, meditation has been there, like an old trusted friend, guiding me, protecting me from circumstances that may have thrown me off center, bringing me back home.

I became a serious meditator in the mid-seventies, while visiting my teacher, Siddha Yoga meditation master Swami Muktananda, known affectionately as Baba.[1] During my stay in his ashram in Ganeshpuri, India, there were multitudes of obstacles that Baba helped me move through, and profound teachings he helped me understand. But the most memorable one was the one he gave me firsthand on the discipline of meditation.

I had meditated off and on prior to going to India, but I hadn't taken it seriously. I was more like a guest, visiting the experience from time to time. It wasn't until I began to sit every morning in the dark, fragrant room beneath the ashram, known as "the cave," that I "moved in," so to speak, and became addicted to this divine practice.

There I'd be, the first one at the door at three in the morning, and the last one to leave two hours later. I would sit and watch the endless stream of thoughts churning away in my mind, and then, as if someone had turned off the switch, all thoughts would dissolve. I would feel my entire body fill with an incredible sense of joy, contentment, and serenity.

As I sat there morning after morning, this marathon of uninterrupted bliss became the highlight of my day. The more habitual I made this practice, the longer I was able to sit and the deeper I went. Time was somewhere off in the distance; my body transcended its physical limitations. Intrigued with this new inner world, I became a spectator to an inner universe that unfolded before me, layer upon layer of resistance exposed. And then, I was able to see something beyond the resistance. Finally, after thirty years of living, I had a glimpse of who I was at the core, the connection to source. There was a comfort unlike any I had ever experienced before—a tangible knowing of who I was. And this *knowing* slowly replaced the constant anxiety I had been accustomed to living with for years.

After leaving the ashram I felt concern, of course, that once I returned home I might not maintain this consistency in my practice. But I am happy to say there is rarely a day that I do not sit, at least for twenty minutes, usually in the morning and at night.

If you have never meditated before, here is a simple introduction. And even if you've been meditating for years, you may want to take a little dip and connect to your source, right now.

A Simple Meditation Practice

First, find a place in your home that is relatively quiet, a place where you won't be disturbed. Move around the room until you resonate with a spot, and place a pillow there. If you prefer not to sit cross-legged on the floor, find a comfortable chair that allows you to keep your back upright, without strain. Place a woolen blanket over the pillow or on the seat of the chair, as it will absorb and amplify the cumulative energy of your meditation practice. Sit comfortably.

Now close your eyes and take a deep breath. Let it out slowly. Take another deep breath and exhale slowly. If you feel any place in your body where there is pain or tension, breathe into the spot a few times and watch the tension dissolve.

Take another deep breath and let it out slowly. Starting with your temples, and moving down to the cheek area, the nose, and around the lips, notice if there is any pressure in your face. Breathe into the tension and let it go. Relax your jaw. Gently check the rest of your body to see if there are any other places where there might be pressure or holding on, and let the tension go.

Bring your attention to your breath. You can repeat the word *Om* on the in-breath and *Om* on the out-breath. Or use another mantra with which you're comfortable or a word that has a quality you need at this time, like *peace* or *love*. Keep repeating your word or your mantra as you settle into the inner space of the Self.

Thoughts will inevitably begin to surface. Don't try to block them. Don't fight them. Just watch your thoughts without getting attached to them. Remember, your mind is simply doing its job—thinking! Without focusing on their content, simply observe the thoughts dancing in front of you. And keep letting the thoughts go—words are birds, flying away. Or imagine your thoughts being carried gently down a river. You're just sitting on the bank of the river, watching.

You will undoubtedly get lost in your thoughts now and again. Keep bringing your attention back to the breath and the word or the mantra you're repeating. Let your attention be drawn to the *sound* of the word or the mantra, the *resonance* of the mantra, inside. The steadiness of being immersed in the breath and repeating *Om* will take you deeper.

When you are comfortable, and your thoughts have slowed down and you are breathing deeply, you can let go of the *Om* and let go of watching the breath and allow yourself to keep letting go of all thoughts and feelings, time and space. Let go of who you are; let go of your surroundings. Let go of everything you know and don't know. Just dive deeper and deeper into the silent well that nourishes you and energizes you and loves you, as you are, unconditionally.

Sit for as long as you like. Meditation often has a twenty-minute internal cycle, so try to sit for at least twenty minutes. Twice a day, if you can.

Meditation as the Foundation

So what does meditation have to do with marketing and public relations?

By starting our day with this practice, we stand firm in our present state of awareness. We become conscious of our thoughts and our emotions. Our decisions come from a place of conviction, rather than from guessing. The banter and chatter about whether we should advertise here, promote ourselves there, collaborate with partners, or build a practice of our own . . . stops. We listen more closely, more attentively, not only to our own thoughts and emotions, but also to the thoughts and emotions of our clients and our customers. Listening to the subtext behind their words provides us with the insight we need to serve them in more meaningful ways. Patience becomes an active, dynamic virtue we perform, rather than an act of passive toleration. And, at those moments when we feel overwhelmed, we are conscious of the imbalance. We step back from the chaos and pause. And in the pause, we know we can sit, get in touch with the source once again, and be guided.

When we are truly in connection with this source, we are in touch with the deepest level of truth, reality, and intention. We become aware of the consequences of our actions. We know when something is not *dharmic*, not a right action, and we become incapable of performing selfish, destructive acts.

The Beginning of Magnetism

The more I travel, the more people I meet who engage in meditation. I notice them right away; they convey a sense of enthusiasm and purpose. They don't dwell in states of negativity, and whatever the nature of their profession, they are filled with a determination and focus. I see it in their eyes, in their body language. I hear it in their speech. It is clear they have worked diligently on their *shenpas*, the word

Buddhist author Pema Chödrön uses to describe the itch, "the irritations that create suffering." [2] They do not respond to themselves or to others with knee-jerk reactions. Rather, they remain present with "the itch," and deal with it in the moment. Until they take into consideration all factors, they do not react. They see the whole picture rather than narrow fragments. When these folks mention to me that they meditate, I can't help but smile. It confirms once again the power we have to mirror and become the magnet for those persons, situations, and opportunities we want to have close to us, and I am grateful.

The Fruits of Meditation

For me, the fruits of meditation have been many. I know that I have transformed into a happier person, no longer taking myself so seriously. I am more careful of the words I use, the food I eat, and the people with whom I associate. I experience longer states of peace and tranquility. And I definitely take better care of my health. But the most profound fruit of meditation is the faint voice inside that gets louder and clearer the longer I sit. This voice, when I listen, guides me toward the improvements I need to make. It's the tuning fork that keeps me in tune, in sync; it lets me know when it's time to move, when it's time to make changes, when it's time to slow down or stop.

Michael Slater, a university professor who has practiced meditation for thirty years, says:

> When I step back from an ego-driven engagement in my professional and personal life, and make even fleeting conscious contact with the pure conscious awareness that is our true nature, life becomes fresh. My enthusiasm returns, and the ability to handle challenges or generate fresh ideas flows naturally. When I try to work from my head alone, I get stuck in my preconceptions

and nothing really new or insightful emerges. When I reach deeper, I have a clearer intuitive awareness of what is worth trying, worth exploring, worth doing.[3]

Steve Palevich, a real-estate investor from Albuquerque, New Mexico, says,

> Meditation for me is like breathing: survival depends on it. At least survival in the form in which I choose to live. Through meditation, I have access to guidance beyond the capability of my mind and beyond the reach of my experiences. This knowing often reveals itself during my working moments with a delightful surety that is undeniable. This in-the-moment and preemptive guidance protects and supports me to such an extent that I would never consider not meditating daily.[4]

In her recent book, *Megatrends 2010: The Rise of Conscious Capitalism*, Patricia Aburdene recounts the story of Bill George, CEO of Minneapolis-based Medtronic, the company that invented pacemakers. Bill started meditating twenty-five years ago. Not only did his private commitment to meditation give him more energy; he amplified Medtronic's corporate consciousness. Bill found that most of his creative ideas came out of meditation. In meditation practice, he would get great clarity about what was really important in the company. During his tenure, Medtronic went from $1.1 billion to $60 billion in corporate value.[5]

The Ultimate Invitation

Meditation is an ongoing process, an internal discovery that never ends. I encourage you to try it, even as an experiment. Watch and see how, day by day, subtle, positive shifts occur. How your concentration improves, how your mood swings become less dramatic, how your intellect becomes keener.

Taking those precious moments to go inside is not always easy; in fact we will find loads of excuses to avoid it. But the truth remains: when we yield to this practice at least once a day and dive into the bliss, then the bliss becomes a bubble, and that bubble protects our every move.

Strike up a love affair with meditation, and see how your life unfolds. Even if you sit for just a few minutes each day and build slowly, your very taste for meditation will grow stronger and allow you to sit longer. Be patient. Like all intimate relationships, meditation has its peaks and valleys, its intensities and expansions. Issues of time and space will collide with the demands of everyday life. Nevertheless, as you return to this divine place day after day, it will become an exquisite home, a place of refuge you will feel extremely safe and cozy living in.

This is not hocus-pocus, nor is it a game. Meditation is a concrete practice that allows us to live more freely in the moment, in the flow of life and its surprising events. The thought-free state that we enter when we meditate connects us to our highest intuition, and paves the way for us to trust that our deepest desires will not only be fulfilled, they will be God's wish for us.

This is the first step of the initiation into magnetism. This is how it all begins.

FOR FURTHER CONTEMPLATION

1. What practice connects you to your source?

   Whether it is meditation or some other practice, contemplate these questions:

2. Does your practice bring you the peace, tranquility, and equanimity you would like to experience? If not, what do you feel would make this experience possible for you? What changes do you need to make so you can have this experience?

3. Has your practice supported you in making decisions, clarifying priorities, leveraging opportunities, or developing effective and satisfying relationships in business as in your personal life?

4. Are there ways you can improve your practice? Would it help to set aside more time, get up earlier, turn off all electronics? Do you need more physical exercise, a walk, different food, stretching exercises or hatha yoga before sitting to meditate? What other actions could you take that would deepen your practice or your experience of it?

5. Do you need the support of other people to maintain your practice? How can you find or build that support? Where do you need to look or what actions do you need to take to help to create that supportive community?

CHAPTER 3

ALIGNING WITH OUR SOUL'S CALLING

Let your mind start a journey through a strange new world.
Leave all thoughts of the world you knew before. Let your soul take
you where you long to be . . . Close your eyes, let your spirit start to
soar, and you'll live as you've never lived before.

— Anonymous

Imagine looking into a crystal ball and seeing exactly what your future is to be and what you would *feel* like once you gained access to it. Now imagine: No ball. Instead, you have a key: the key that opens the door to this knowledge whenever you want it. To go there, all you have to do is to ask yourself a few questions.

That would be pretty cool, right? Better than a crystal ball. This is what happens when we align ourselves with the call of the soul.

Aligning with Our Soul's Calling is the second step of the initiation into magnetism. It is a vision quest, a wondrous ride we take to discover our hidden directions and desires. Full of surprises and unexpected twists and turns, this journey is one that cannot be approached through the intellect. In fact, it bypasses the analytical mind and ego entirely, enabling us to connect with our highest intuition from the purest place. Like the divination techniques of the *I Ching*, the Tarot, and the Runes, which reveal our unconscious thoughts, the quest to align with our soul's calling bares our deepest longings and helps us define and outline our future. It energizes our soul's destiny, and makes it visible to us. Unlike divination techniques, there is no need for any outside reference—no cards, no yarrow stalks, no stones, no coins. All it takes is us!

LEARN TO KNOW—INSTEAD OF GUESS

No one wants to make "mistakes" or waste precious time or money. We want answers right away! Just like we want to find the magic pill that will cure our ailments, or the quick fix that will dissolve our mental, physical, or emotional pain. We'll even pay psychics and clairvoyants to reveal our future to us. But wouldn't you prefer to enter into this place of wisdom on your own?

I used to get incredibly frustrated when I didn't *know* the answer to something immediately. I would try to be patient but, ever restless, I would force a response, even if it wasn't time for the answer to be revealed. And then there'd be times when I thought I'd made the right decision, but I hadn't. Since taking part in this exercise, I have a deeper trust in knowing when a decision needs to be made, when to rein in, and when to charge ahead.

Never having glimpsed our future creates hesitation and doubt, as if a dark cloud were hovering over our every move. This uncertainty prevents us from being patient, acting spontaneously, or taking risks, and, in fact, goads us to repeat fruitless cyclical habits. When we know on a deep, profound level what our soul is calling for us to *be* in this moment—and *become* in the future—we walk through life with a certain determination and confidence. We stand taller; we speak with more sincerity and conviction. As with the fruits we receive from meditation, there is no question as to what path we should take, where we should invest, if we should invest, or with whom we should associate. When we are connected with how we want to feel, through the insight of our vision, we *know* exactly what direction to go in.

ALIGNING WITH OUR FUTURE

The "Aligning with Our Soul's Calling" exercise was first introduced in my book *Creating an Abundant Practice*. Because of its value and transformative potential, I feel it is imperative to present it anew here.

I have introduced this guided quest to thousands of people who have participated in my workshops and consultations. I have watched as their lives have expanded and their businesses have taken off, exceeding all expectations. I'll never forget one woman who took a workshop in upstate New York. She walked up to me after the vision quest and said, "Thank you very much, Andrea. I just saw my entire future in incredible detail and I am blown away. This was all I needed." Before she flew out the door, she said, "Keep the money I paid for the workshop. I'm also going to send you a check to cover two of my friends who really need to take your workshop and experience this exercise." What could I say?

Then there was Jeffrey, an acupuncturist from Hawaii. He had always wanted to live by the ocean and set up his healing practice there. He told me he had searched for five years to find a house he could afford. Two days after going on the vision quest during a consultation, he found the house of his dreams and moved in shortly afterward. When I asked him, "Why do you think you found this house so fast?" he said, "I had always seen this house in my dreams, but I'd never experienced the feeling associated with it—how I would *feel* living in it. As soon as I did, the vision and the feelings aligned themselves and I found the house. It was awesome!" [1]

Are You Ready?

There are three ways in which you can take this journey. You can read the rest of this chapter and go on the voyage by yourself. You can invite a friend to do it with you and take turns reading it to each other. Or you can purchase the CD at www.HolisticPR.com and have me walk you through it.

My suggestion would be to read through the exercise first, become familiar with it, and then decide which way you'd like to participate.

Aligning with Your Soul's Calling: The Exploration

Please get a journal or a writing pad, and a pencil or pen. Draw a straight line down the center of a clean page. At the top of the left-hand column, write the word *Feelings*. At the top on the right, write the word *Visions*. You can use these columns to write down your feelings and your visions as they come up for you.

If you have a friend walking you through the exercise, have them write down your experiences as you speak them aloud, so you don't have to break your train of thought.

You may want to create a relaxing environment by turning off the telephone, placing a "do not disturb" sign on your door, lighting some incense, and eliminating all potential distractions. Now place the paper and pen close by and take a comfortable posture.

When you're comfortable, close your eyes and take a deep breath; fill your lungs with all the wonderful air that surrounds you.

Let it out slowly.

Take another deep breath.

Allow your breath to exhale slowly.

Take a moment and think about the day you've had so far. As

you reflect on the day, get in touch with the feelings that come up for you. Take your time. Really own these feelings. Breathe into them, again and again.

Take another deep breath. On the next exhalation, allow these feelings to leave your body and dissolve. With each exhalation, continue to watch your thoughts and feelings melt away. Let go of all cares and concerns, and allow yourself to enter a state of quiet inner freedom. Immersed in this state of beginner's mind, you're ready for your journey.

Now, I'd like you to take a huge leap, into the most magnificent future you can imagine for yourself.

If you were given total permission to dream this magnificent future, what would the vision look like?

Allow your imagination to soar beyond the room, beyond time, beyond space. And know that you have a choice: to walk through one of five doors. You can walk through the awful door; the okay door; the good door; the great door; or the awesome door.

Pick a door.

There are no parameters, no boundaries in this vision.

Once you have selected the door you want to step through, imagine a fairy godmother, a benevolent being, appearing before you with a magic wand, granting you all your wishes. See what your most incredible future could be like if you allowed it to manifest right now.

Take your time. Really see this future.

Breathe into it.

You may see this vision in great detail, or you may have a simple impression of light. You may have a metaphoric image, an experience with words, or intuitions. Whatever comes up for you is perfect. Do not judge the journey; just go with it!

When the vision, or the sense of this future, and the feelings associated with this vision are clear for you, write them down in their respective columns: *Feelings* and *Visions*.

Take several more deep breaths and let them out slowly.

Now imagine your life ONE YEAR from today. Once again, select one of the doors to walk through: the awful door; the okay door; the good door; the great door; or the awesome door. See what your life could be like one year from today.

See this vision in as much detail as possible. See what changes have taken place from the previous year. What has stayed the same?

Feel the quality of the year. What feelings are coming up for you as you experience this year, one year from today?

When the vision and the feelings are clear for you, please write them down.

Breathe in deeply again; let it out slowly.

Take another deep breath and let it out slowly.

Now let yourself move forward in time. Imagine your life THREE YEARS from today. Select one of the five doors—the awful door, the okay door, the good door, the great door, or the awesome door—and walk through it.

What is your life three years from today? What changes have been made?

See your life in as much detail as possible. Move into your deepest yearnings.

When this vision is clear for you, get in touch with the feelings associated with it and write them down.

THE SCIENCE OF SPIRITUAL MARKETING

Breathe in deeply again; let it out slowly.

Take another deep breath and allow your breath to exhale slowly.

Now, imagine your life FIVE YEARS from today. Select one of the five doors, and walk through. Visualize what your life could be like in five years' time.

Step into the picture and look at the changes, and the places where things have stayed the same. See how close this year's vision is to the one you jumped out into in the first vision. It doesn't matter if the visions are the same. Just see what's there for you. Take everything in. When the vision is clear, get in touch with how you are feeling, and when you are ready, write down the vision and the feeling connected with it.

Breathe in deeply again; let it out slowly.

Take another deep breath and let it out slowly.

Now, I'd like you to imagine your life as if it were your VERY LAST DAY on this earth. You are about to leave your body. Walk through one of those doors.

Where are you? What are you doing? Are you surrounded by friends and loved ones, or are you alone and content?

What is the state of your body, mind, and spirit? Have you accomplished all that you wanted? Are there any regrets?

Are you excited about leaving, ready for the next excursion to begin?

Experience the inner feelings as well as the outer circumstances.

When this vision and the feelings are clear for you, open your eyes and write down what you have experienced.

If one or more of your future visions were not clear, do not be concerned. It may not be time for you to see them. The important thing is that you have a strong sense of what each of the visions *feels* like.

From this moment on, you will want to remember how you felt in these visions, as these are the feelings that you want to resonate with from now on. The more you connect energetically with these feelings, the sooner you will draw to you those people, events, and synchronicities that will support you in bringing your vision into real time.

And you may want to keep in mind, if there is any part of your future that you are unhappy about, you can change it. If you see yourself as an old lady or an old man who may not be in the best of health, you can change the vision to an elder who is serene and happy. If you see yourself working at different jobs before finding the right one, you can envision the right one and feel what it would be like to be earning a living in that profession—how getting up every morning and dressing for that job would make you feel.

From now on, stay connected to these vibratory sensations. Allow them to be the golden thread that weaves through all your thoughts and experiences. Let them be your source of support as you move through your days. And if, by chance, you lose touch with them, take a close look at what you might be creating instead. Ask yourself, "Is this in alignment with how I want to *be* and *feel?*" Then, gently return to them.

It's About the Feeling

How you *feel* while you are connected to your future is key. It is only by connecting to these feelings, as often as you can, that you find the courage to make the necessary leaps that will change your present.

Here is an example: Early on in my career, I was making a meager living and hardly had any money to advertise for my workshops. So, I never did. It was a pattern I had gotten used to, and then just stuck with even after I began to make a good living.

On one occasion, some years into the process, I was scheduled to present a workshop in Oakland, California. The workshop was not as full as I had hoped it would be and it was only a week away. That day, I received a phone call from a radio show in the Oakland area asking me if I wanted to be on a program that catered to hundreds of small-business owners and entrepreneurs—clearly my audience.

The producer said she had heard about my work and thought her audience would be very interested in spiritual marketing and knowing about the upcoming workshop. She also said it would cost me $350 to be on the show. My knee-jerk reaction was to say "No, absolutely not!" But for some reason, I told her I would think about it. She gave me two hours to make up my mind; the show was scheduled to air first thing in the morning. I told her I'd call her back soon.

I walked into my meditation room, sat down on my *asana*, my woolen meditation seat, and began to clear my head and pray for clarity.

When my meditation was over, I asked myself, "So, Andrea, what's the vision for this workshop?" I saw the room in Oakland filled with people interested in what I had to say, having breakthroughs, laughing, and interacting with each other. "How are you feeling in this vision?" I asked. Fantastic, thrilled that so many people were learning and having fun, changing paradigms. "So, what is it going to take for you to fill the workshop, and experience those feelings?" Well, I guess I should do the radio show.

As soon as I got in touch with the vision of the workshop and the feelings associated with it, I knew the show was a gift, regardless of the fear and the pattern I'd been attached to in the past.

I got up, called the producer, and told her I wanted to do the interview. The next morning, during the show, thirty people called in with questions. Within a week, sixty people had signed up for the workshop. Seven people who could not attend called me for consultations. Do you think it was worth the $350 investment?

This is what happens when we move beyond our conditioned beliefs and emotions and connect with our subtle instinctual receptors. The more we live in this place of trusting our feelings, beyond our limited habitual awareness, the more those opportunities and synchronicities will become present to us.

It's About the Vision

The power of this process lies in the union of vision with feeling. As important as it is to hold on to the feeling, we need to hold on to and connect with the vision as well.

Here's another example: Maria is an actress. She ran up to me one evening at an event and excitedly shared with me that she was about to produce her first play. "I just signed the contract," she said. "I now have the legal rights to launch the play in New Mexico, which means I can showcase it in Santa Fe, Taos, and Albuquerque." Then, Maria asked me what I thought the best strategy would be to promote the show. "What's your vision for the production?" I asked her. "Well," she said, "I want to use it as a showcase for my work as an actress. That way, I can get more parts in movies."

Now, although it is true that New Mexico is becoming quite a little film state, the majority of films that come to the Land of Enchantment are still cast in L.A. and New York. So I asked Maria, "Why did you agree to produce the play only in New Mexico? Why not get the rights to produce the play in New York and in L.A., where the casting directors are? How many casting people will fly to New

Mexico to see you in this play? Or to see *any* play, for that matter?"

Maria hadn't realized how she had pigeonholed herself by negotiating the rights of the play only in New Mexico. Because Maria had been an actress for so many years and was used to focusing so intently on the character she was developing, she didn't see the bigger picture—the picture that was needed for the entire production, and her role in it.

This was a huge lesson for Maria, and for all of us. Because it's not *just* the feelings we want to connect with. It is, in addition, the ultimate vision for our project or endeavor that we need to hold in our mind, and then we take action from that place.

STAYING ALIGNED

When we connect with the deep internal flame of genuine passion and undeniable inspiration that is inside us, we reside in the place of knowing that our future is real, standing right before us. When we know that all we have to do is walk into it, feel it, and it will be ours, we can trust that our next steps will propel us to live more fully in the present moment.

As we focus on this future truth and *feel* ourselves manifesting it, transformation will occur. Our present takes on a whole new quality—one that includes faith and trust, wisdom and grace. As we walk forward into the vision of our future, every moment of our life, *right now*, is transformed. We are empowered not only to make the right choices, but to be present in a whole new way.

Aligning with Our Soul's Calling is the second step in the initiation process. It complements our practice of meditation, our connection to source, and supports us in the evolution of bringing that connection into tangible manifestation in the outer realities of our life, and in our business.

FOR FURTHER CONTEMPLATION

1. What was the initial vision you had for your soul's calling, the one you stepped out into at the very beginning? What were the feelings associated with that vision?

2. When you stepped back and walked into the vision one year from today, what did you see? What were the feelings that surfaced?

3. When you saw your life two years later, what changes had occurred? What feelings were associated with that vision?

4. In your vision for the fifth year, how close was it to the one you jumped out into originally? What were the feelings associated with it?

5. When you stepped into your vision for your last day on earth, what came up for you? How did you feel on this last day?

6. Are you owning each of your visions and the feelings associated with them? Can you hold on to these feelings and trust that they will move you toward your soul's calling?

CHAPTER 4

THE THREE STAGES OF CREATIVITY

*Nothing in the universe is created, preserved, or destroyed
without the mutual agreement and approval of the three aspects
of the Supreme Being, for they are unitedly essential for the
production and reproduction of all forms of life.*

— Author unknown

There I was, attending a screenwriting lecture given by Cynthia Whitcomb at the Santa Fe Screenwriting Conference, when, all of a sudden, Cynthia nonchalantly mentioned the mythological Hindu triad of Brahmā, Vishnu, and Shiva, and how she uses the triad as a metaphor for the three stages of creativity.[1] *Wow,* I thought, practically jumping out of my seat, *what a concept!* As a student of Eastern meditation, a teacher, and a writer, always wanting to excel in the creative process, I was only too anxious to hear how these seemingly unrelated concepts correlated. The more I listened, the more I understood that we are constantly moving in and out of these stages, shifting our attention, getting lost, continually rebalancing around a center that is always in motion. And how, if we use this triad as a guide, we can gain more insight into our own creative endeavors, to establish balance and equanimity.

Completely intrigued and in the midst of writing this book, with no time to get stuck in any one of these stages, I decided to research these ancient images, delve deeper into their history, and see how they could serve us all.

A LITTLE HISTORY

You may have seen a picture of this three-in-one image at one time or another in a history book, in an exhibit of Eastern art, or while watching a Bollywood film. Perhaps you've seen this triad at a New Age bookstore, or a museum, but never gave it much thought. In the West it's sometimes called the Hindu "Trinity": in the East it's known as the *trimurti*.[2]

Familiar as these images had seemed to me through the years of yoga and meditation, as I researched them I began to see them through new eyes. No longer were they simply esoteric, mysterious images from posters and sculptures. They were now taking on personalities with individual characteristics. They became practical tools and reminders as to how I expend my energy, how I waste time, and how I can be more efficient. The more conscious I became of their attributes, the more they stirred and encouraged my creativity to flourish. As I explored these images in more detail, I understood how they can guide us to greater effectiveness, and ease, in our own creative process.

Let's take a look at their origins.

The Origin of the Trimurti

The word *trimurti* means "having three forms." Each form is recognized individually as Brahmā, Vishnu, and Shiva. In Hindu mythology, while they each represent a different aspect of creation, they are also seen as different ways to experience the one Supreme Being.[3]

In principle, each of these forces or images is equal to the others in power and influence. In the classic representation, the three faces emerge from one single column, like three blossoms from the same stem, each looking in a different direction. Brahmā, the Creator, looks to the left; Vishnu, the Sustainer, looks straight ahead; and Shiva, the Destroyer, looks to the right. These faces not only symbolize the Supreme Deity whose essence pervades the entire universe as the pulsation of creation, they also encompass the entire spectrum of our *inner* universe and illustrate how our inner state plays itself out in the world.

In the pages that follow, I describe each aspect of the Triad, and include stories that depict how we mortals can easily get caught up in any one of these stages. In these stories, I use the word "devotee" in a tongue-in-cheek way to illustrate how we become devoted to and invested in our addiction to a particular stage.

The stories are all true. I have simply changed the names to protect the players, innocent and guilty alike. As you read through them, it may be an interesting observation for you to see which of these devotees remind you of yourself, or of someone you know.

BRAHMĀ

The word *brahmā* is from a Sanskrit root meaning "expansion," "development," "bubbling up." Brahmā is the personification of creation.[3] The Brahmā aspect is the stage we settle into when we want to envision, imagine, and tune in to our divine inspiration.

In traditional iconography, Brahmā is depicted as red in color, with four heads and four arms. His hands hold a rosary, a sacrificial ladle, and the Vedas, a collection of ancient scriptural texts. Brahmā is said to be the origin of the Vedas, which, according to Hindu mythology, the ancient sages actually heard resounding from his being.

The world is said to exist for one *kalpa*, an incalculably long era that forms one day in the life of Brahmā. At the end of a kalpa, the whole world is destroyed, or reabsorbed into the primordial point of origin. It is said that Brahmā then falls asleep for one night, a night that is as long as a kalpa. When he awakens, he recreates the world. This process is repeated for one hundred of his years, the life span of one incarnation of Brahmā. Then everything dissolves into its unmanifest state and the whole process is repeated unendingly.

The unbent bow he is sometimes shown holding suggests that the action of Brahmā is within. He prepares for the deed, centering himself, aligning himself before moving into any outward activity. Brahmā is the in-breath and the pause that is the effortless drawing back of the bow.

The Brahmā stage is pure, magical, and untainted. It is the stage we enter into when we meditate, contemplate, or go inside and align ourselves with our vision. It is the stage we explore when we imagine all our possibilities and desire our thoughts to expand. The Brahmā stage is essential for initiating any creative course of action.

Here is an example of a devotee of Brahmā, one who has become lost in the Brahmā stage.

A Devotee of Brahmā

James Cannon always had great ideas regarding his life's work. He dreamed of traveling to foreign lands, making documentary films, starting a political newspaper, and building dome houses. He had envisioned doing all of them . . . one day. He would take long walks with his son along the river near their house, and they would dream their dreams together.

There was only one problem. James rarely took any steps to implement the projects he dreamed about. He refused to sign up for classes at the local college or research courses he could enroll in. He never met with other filmmakers or apprenticed with a production company. Instead, he took odd jobs that were never truly satisfying, and made just enough money to pay the rent. He'd come home from work and complain to his son about not having enough money to start any of the businesses he was interested in. In other words, James was stuck in the Brahmā stage, and could not find his way out.

We have all dreamed of doing exciting things, we all have those goals we want to accomplish before we leave this earth, but how often do we really see them through?

Brahmā is an important stage to revel in. It is the first aspect of creativity and it is essential for creative beings and creation itself. It's the stage in which we pause and dream before we create the picture on canvas, before we start our composition, take our next step in business, or write our book. But our time in Brahmā has its limits, and those limits are different for everyone. You may want to think about what those limits are for you.

And then there is the call from Vishnu. Are we aware of that call? The one we must respond to so we can put our vision into action.

VISHNU

Vishnu is "the all-pervader," "the worker," "the accomplisher," and the second face of the Hindu triad. As the preserver of the universe, Vishnu is the active upholder, the rescuer; as the cosmic force, he is likened to the ocean. He is known as Narayana, the one who moves on the waters. Vishnu is intimately connected with the path of *dharma*, right action, that which maintains humanity and offers salvation through faithfulness to the paths of responsibility. Dharma is that which sustains.

Vishnu is represented as dark and mysterious, the deep color of clouds that bring rain. Four-armed, he is often seen dressed in yellow garments. In one hand he holds a club, in another a conch shell, in the third a discus, and in the fourth a lotus. The river Ganga, pouring down from its source in the Himalaya, is said to flow from Vishnu's feet. He is often portrayed as resting on a coiled serpent, afloat on the cosmic ocean. Vishnu's abode, Vaikuntha, shimmers with gold and jewels.[4]

THE SCIENCE OF SPIRITUAL MARKETING

Whenever there is an imbalance between good and evil on the earth, Vishnu reestablishes the balance. Vishnu represents the stage of operation: putting the vision into action, watering the field, actively nurturing the creation so that our visions grow to their fullest potential.

It's possible, though, to be lost in the Vishnu stage.

A Devotee of Vishnu

Karen Steiner owned a beautiful restaurant in Hawaii. It was a popular hangout with delicious raw-food cuisine, beloved by locals and flocked to by tourists from far and wide. Karen worked hard every day, inventing new recipes, chopping, blending, managing, bookkeeping, and at times even waitressing. She was a great chef and a wonderful boss, and her employees loved her.

The difficulty was that Karen did not know how to delegate or how to ask other people to support her. She never took the time to pause and envision what the restaurant could be like if she stepped back from it and imagined the larger possibility.

Stuck in the Vishnu stage, Karen was blinded by the work ethic she was taught as a child. She neglected the Brahmā stage of visioning the bigger picture. She also never moved into the Shiva stage of letting go. Karen was stuck in Vishnu and unable to see the light at the end of the restaurant.

SHIVA

Shiva is the destroyer. And yet his name literally means "the auspicious one." He is the aspect of release and regeneration. As the third face of the triad, Shiva represents the darkness of involution and the return to origins. He is said to be "the angry one," and at the same time, he is known as "he who is easily pleased." Since creation follows destruction, Shiva is regarded as a reproductive power, restoring that which has been dissolved.

Shiva is portrayed in many forms. His most common depiction is as a dark-skinned ascetic with a blue throat, seated cross-legged on a tiger skin, hair matted and coiled on his head, adorned with a snake and a crescent moon. The third eye in the center of his forehead is always closed, opening only to annihilate evil. A garland of skulls, *rudraksha* beads, or a twined serpent is draped around his neck, and bracelets of serpents adorn his arms and wrists. He is the master of all forces.

In one hand, Shiva holds his trident, to which is tied a double-headed drum or *damaru*. In another hand, he holds a conch shell, and in the third, a rudraksha rosary, a club, or a bow. One hand is empty, raised in a gesture of blessing and protection. Around his waist he wears a tiger skin or leopard skin, and his bare upper body is smeared with ashes, befitting one who has burned away all attachments.[5]

The Shiva aspect is that of letting go, destroying or dissolving past actions. As we perform our every action with effort and grace, we watch the dance of creation, perseverance, and dissolution. We learn through Shiva to let go and clear the deck for the next lightning bolt to strike.

Here's what happens when someone is lost in the Shiva stage.

A DEVOTEE OF SHIVA

Sara Langley was a born entrepreneur. Even during her teens, as a Girl Scout, Sara could sell more peanut-butter cookies than anyone in her troop. She was always fair in business, and had a strong sense of integrity. But as Sara matured, her entrepreneurial skills became limited by her obsession with the Shiva stage: she always let go too soon.

Sara was in her thirties when she purchased a small manufacturing company that produced natural, nontoxic laundry detergent. She was off to a running start. After a brief showing at a natural-products expo, mothers were interested, stores were interested, and she was establishing accounts with local and regional stores. Soon after the expo, Sara experienced a financial challenge. She felt overwhelmed with how much product she needed to order and was afraid to go into debt. Instead of seeking guidance and speaking to other entrepreneurs who might have had similar challenges, she let go of all the hard work she had put into the business and sold it. The people to whom she sold the business did their due diligence, sought out the help they needed, and the company is now worth millions.

It happened again when she started a magazine for women, only this time the obstacle Sara met with was personal. She and her boyfriend split up and she was an emotional wreck. Instead of seeking the help she needed to try to resolve the relationship or get through the breakup, she became anxious and unstable. Instead of persevering, she let go of the magazine. Ruled by the Shiva aspect, she was never able to manifest her dreams to fulfillment by seeing them through.

After hearing the following story, I felt compelled to include it as the antithesis of the Shiva devotee.

An Aversion to Shiva

George Sharp worked for thirty-five years as the owner of a construction business. He had seventy employees and an admirable reputation for building quality homes and shopping centers. George had created such a strong brand that when it came time to sell his business, he was able to sell it quickly and make a huge profit.

Even though George had sold his company and received the generous amount he'd asked for, he was still attached to the business. He was unable to move into the Shiva stage of letting go, allowing another door to open. Hired as a consultant for the firm, he hounded the new owners, micromanaging their business. His behavior drove the owners crazy. George's clinging to the business never gave the new owners the freedom they needed to try new ideas, to fall and pick themselves up. Nor did this behavior give George the freedom to move on in his life. His clinging not only destroyed his relationship with the new owners, it broke up his marriage and turned George into a very unhappy man.

Because George wouldn't let his old creation dissolve, he never moved into the Brahmā stage of fruitful imagination so that a new creation could take form.

Bringing the Triad into Our Lives

Understanding the three stages of creativity can be an incredible asset to our creative development—or we can get so caught up in any one of them that we lose our way and go off on tangents. It's all about staying conscious and understanding that each face of the triad merges into the others; each contains the next, and they are not to be seen as separate entities. When we really get that each stage is moving, shifting, forming and dissolving into the next in a constantly dynamic motion without ceasing, we begin to honor these stages. We see that they ultimately give us the image of a fluid poise, pointing the way to restoring equilibrium when something in our creative process has become unbalanced.

By acknowledging these cycles in our lives, we develop flexibility and balance. We see the necessity for each stage in turn. We begin to witness the indulgences, the imbalances, when we let ourselves linger in one extreme or another. Knowing how these cycles manifest, we are quickly brought back to center—and learn the dance of Nataraj.

THE DANCE OF DELIGHT

The enchanting image of Shiva Nataraj, "Lord of the Dance," represents all stages of the triad. He reminds us to engage in all aspects of his ecstatic movement with grace, harmony, and motion, and not to shy away from its rhythmic force.

Nataraj is forever serene and smiling, his left foot elegantly raised, his right foot effortlessly at rest, subduing the prostrate figure of the demon of unawareness. Braided and bejeweled, his matted locks whirl as he dances within an arch of flames, the endless cycle of birth and death. The skull adorning his hair symbolizes his conquest over death. The holy river Ganges, pouring down from heaven, is caught in the net of his locks. His third eye flashes forth his omniscience, insight, and enlightenment. And all this whirling rests on a lotus pedestal, tranquil and immaculate, the source of the creative force of the universe.[6]

Nataraj's state is the place we want to play in. He is the ultimate dancer, constantly moving in and out of the three stages with graceful delight.

FUSING THE TRIAD AND NATARAJ

The Hindu triad and Shiva Nataraj are both reminders of the center in the midst of movement, the dynamic equanimity that embraces all phases of the creative cycle. By implementing these qualities, we can become centered and engaged in the flow of life, even as the world spins around us. No longer either fearing time or throwing it away, we honor it. No longer victims of unconscious behavior, we jump off the wheel of destructive archetypes and move into an ebb and flow that shows us how we can be practical, creative, and skillful. We can experience deeper states of pleasure in our daily activities, while joining Nataraj in the cosmic dance of delicious consciousness.

The Three Stages of Creativity is the third step of the initiation into magnetism. When we bring these stages into steadiness, we are able to move with flexibility and fearlessness through the next step: Moving Beyond Our Comfort Zones.

FOR FURTHER CONTEMPLATION

1. What does the process of creation mean to you?

2. What emotions come up for you when you are creative?

3. How do the three stages of creativity manifest in your life?

4. Are you prone to working in the Brahmā stage? If so, what is your behavior when you are in this stage?

5. Do you work predominantly in the Vishnu stage? If so, how does this stage affect your life?

6. Do you tend to work in the Shiva stage? How does this manifest in your behavior and what are the consequences?

7. Are you able to move in and out of these stages gracefully? If not, what are the blocks preventing you from doing so? Are there actions you could take that would support you in moving through the obstacles into grace and ease?

8. When was the last time you were "in the flow"? Dancing like Nataraj? What did it feel like? What changes do you need to make in order to live and dance in this state more often?

CHAPTER 5

MOVING BEYOND OUR COMFORT ZONES

You just need to be a flea against injustice. Enough committed fleas
biting strategically can make even the biggest dog uncomfortable
and transform even the biggest nation.

— Marian Wright Edelman

While taking a leisurely drive from California to Santa Fe, I listened to a book on tape, *The Orchid Thief*, by Susan Orleans. You may remember it as the book that Nicholas Cage's character in the movie *Adaptation* was trying to adapt as a screenplay. In the book, the author describes the world of orchid fanatics: the growers, the buyers, the thieves, and the lovers. In infinite detail, she describes the varieties of orchids, their texture, their color, and the best climate for them to thrive in. It was more than I ever needed to know about orchids. Still, it was a long ride from L.A. to Santa Fe and I was fascinated by this intriguing tale.

The reason I bring up *The Orchid Thief* in the context of spiritual marketing is that listening to the story of these fanatical orchid lovers struck a chord in my psyche. It triggered the realization that many of us walk around every day ensconced in our own little worlds, without the slightest understanding or compassion for other people's worlds. And because we feel so safe and comfortable, unthreatened, inside the groove we have dug ourselves into, we limit our exposure and narrow our field of opportunity. And then we wonder why we feel stuck and our businesses don't prosper.

In the consulting world, we call this *the manager's box*. It's the syndrome of the manager who runs a specific department and fails to see the importance of networking, listening to his cohorts, or trying new things. Instead, he stays within the confines of his comfort zone and the department never flourishes.

This kind of myopic behavior has deeper implications than just our inability to have an open mind; it brings to the surface our selfishness, our failure to listen, and the limits of our compassion for others. We may ask ourselves, where do these limitations come from? Is this an individual shortcoming, or have we learned this from our families, the media, or the political climate? Do we want to live our life within these margins, or can we choose to be another way? Demonstrating concern and kindness for others is not a weakness; rather, it is a sign of integrity, a posture that strengthens the heart.

WALKING IN SOMEONE ELSE'S SHOES

Alexandra Katehakis, a therapist in Los Angeles, discovered a way for people to enhance individual empathy and break out of limiting self-concepts. She presents a workshop she calls Walking In Your Shoes (WIYS).[1]

WIYS takes place in a group setting, where members of the group ask to be *walked*. One member volunteers to *walk* either side-by-side or behind another person. The facilitator guides the *walker* to listen instinctively to the impulses of the body-mind of the person being walked, and thus the walker becomes the other person. As they walk together, the walker is verbally reporting the other person's thoughts, feelings, and sensations.

As people *walk* and are *walked* by others, participants begin to open up and receive information about each other. One group member might have a sense of personally knowing another even though the two have not previously met. As the walker walks in the other person's shoes, both feel more at ease, more open, and more sensitive to each other.

What I love about the WIYS process is that it demands a willingness to explore the unfamiliar and listen to someone else's heart. Now informed by a greater wisdom that transcends our ordinary experience, we challenge the notion that we are separate; it shows us tangibly that we can move from narrow-mindedness into broader perceptions.

LISTENING TO OTHERS

A woman called my office not too long ago, wanting help with her marketing materials. We didn't hit it off at first. She had an edge to her manner that pushed my buttons; maybe what bothered me was the fact that I saw a part of *myself* in her. Thinking this was not a ride I wanted to go on, I recommended that she find someone else to support her.

Days went by before I heard a little voice inside me say, *Call her back. She needs your help.* I reluctantly listened to the voice, called her back, and was surprised to hear her apologize for being so difficult the last time we'd spoken.

She told me she had gone through a very challenging time. Her husband had died, her house had burned down, and she'd lost everything she owned. The story went on and on, each episode more devastating than the last. The more I listened, the more I could hear her pain, and the more I regretted my inability to hear it the first time she'd called. After she told me about the work she wanted to offer the world, which was coaching people through trauma, my resistance dissolved and my heart melted.

We ended up working together for several months, opening up more and more to each other. I loved working with her and learned quite a bit about working with trauma patients. In hindsight, if I had stayed in my own world and not challenged myself to see someone else's perspective, I would not have had this rich experience. Nor would we have created the marketing materials she needed, or produced the wealth she now enjoys.

Cultural Narrowness

When you think about it, how many wars have started and lasted for centuries because of our inability to see someone else's perspective? We don't have to look very far. Pick up a newspaper! Turn on the news! Look at our religious boundaries, our belief systems, the idea that God appears in only one form, and the pervasive nonacceptance of other paths. Have we not seen enough Holy Wars? It's not religion per se that perpetuates the violence, but an unhealthy narrow-mindedness that seeks to use ideology to control other people's thinking. It is this attitude that keeps us from experiencing our most fundamental freedoms. This immovable stance that we righteously uphold deadens the human spirit and creates robotic behavior, not the freedom of conscious thinkers.

Peter Bergen, a news correspondent for CNN, recently stated, "The reason the United States is disliked by other countries is because we literally do not care what other countries think of us. . . . Not everyone sees the world as we do." [2]

Caring is a critical component of our essential humanity. Another word for this kind of caring is *compassion*.

COMPASSION

Why do we need to have compassion? Perhaps one of the most eminent authorities on the subject, His Holiness the Fourteenth Dalai Lama of Tibet, can shed some light:

> Compassion is a universal responsibility for the feeling of other people's suffering just as we feel our own. . . . We must recognize that all beings want the same thing we want. This is the way to achieve a true understanding, unfettered by artificial consideration.
>
> The true acceptance of the principle of democracy requires that we think and act in terms of the common good. Compassion requires a commitment to personal sacrifice and the neglect of egotistical desires. . . . Accepting responsibility and maintaining respect for others will leave all concerned at peace.[3]

It's true. Having compassion for ourselves and others creates better relationships. The question is, how can we remain sensitive to other people's needs *and* stay in our own power? How can we move out of our comfort zones and stretch ourselves to try new things, add to society in beneficial ways? One way is to cultivate the qualities of the *positive deviant*.

WHAT IS A POSITIVE DEVIANT?

According to Marshall Thurber, attorney, real-estate developer, businessman, author, presenter, and founder of Success Secrets of the 21st Century and the Positive Deviant Network, a positive deviant is a person who constantly breaks the mold. Positive deviants move away from the norm, challenging themselves and others to see the world differently. They are highly passionate people with a high regard for moral and social purpose. They know there is more than one right answer. In fact, they know there are multiple answers. Positive deviants move *toward* what they want, not away from what they don't want; they see failure as a step closer to their goals rather than a cause for depression because they didn't "win" the first time out.[4]

Rapid cognition provides positive deviants with the ability to move from micro to macro as they focus on the bigger picture rather than on the immediate obstacle. They perturb the system, knowing that this will increase the likelihood of breakthrough; they constantly refine their techniques by exploring what is happening on the cutting edge. Positive deviants follow their internal compass, dance to the beat of their own drum, and are not swayed by traditional convention.

In fact, their motto is: All the dogs barking up the wrong tree don't make it the right tree.

When we see leaders who have led with social and moral justice, the businesses they've created, the artists they have become, perhaps it's time *we* adopt some of the positive-deviant qualities they've imbibed.

Rosa Parks, an African American seamstress, refused to relinquish her seat to a white man on a city bus in Montgomery, Alabama, in 1955 and sparked sit-down strikes for equal rights throughout the South and across the nation.

Martin Luther King received the Nobel Peace Prize and the Presidential Medal of Freedom for his unwavering determination to promote nonviolence.

Frida Kahlo never held back. She went on painting, even holding the paintbrush in her teeth as she lay in a body cast after a streetcar accident that left her permanently disabled.

Al Gore, in the wake of his defeat in the 2000 election, reset the course of his life to focus on an all-out effort to help save the planet from irreversible change.

I'm sure you can think of other high-profile positive deviants, as well as people who may not be recognized by mainstream media.

Lane Houk, for example. Founder and national program director of the Herocare program in Fort Myers, Florida, Lane may not be as famous as the positive deviants we've just listed. Still, he moved out of his comfort zone by leaving his profession as a realtor. He saw how frustrating and time-consuming it was for local "heroes"—teachers, firefighters, police officers, soldiers, nurses, social workers—to look for and buy homes, locate loans, reduce debt, and research insurance companies. Seeing the fragmentation and time spent locating these services motivated Lane to come up with a service that brought together banks, realtors, mortgage lenders, insurance companies, and educational institutions. He created a seamless process and an umbrella of services that connects all the dots, and all this with no cost to the employers of these local heroes.[5]

In some fashion, the individuals we admire all had to move out of their comfort zones in order to create something beneficial and lasting. In so doing, they perturbed the system. They became "perturbators." Sounds a bit naughty, right? *Perturbation*, the dictionary tells us, means the disturbance of a course; a shift in the motion of a celestial body produced by some force additional to that which causes its regular motion. In his or her own way, each of these individuals has disbanded the structure, changed the form, and created a new course.

At some point in our lives, we will be faced with having to conjure the courage to become perturbators. What else is life about, anyway? Some people are quite content being on the same course day after day. They wake up, go to work, earn a paycheck, eat, and go to bed every night. They follow "the program" without deviating. The question is, is this kind of life enough for you? Perhaps it is. If it isn't, it may be time for you to re-think where you are. Step out, reach out, leave the comfortable groove you have dug yourself into. Challenge yourself to do what you love. How much time do you think you have to make a difference, to help make this planet a little better than when you entered it?

THE WE–I PARADOX

Many times in our marketing approaches, and in our personal lives, we think we are serving the *WE* (the collective us), when in fact we are only serving and protecting the *I* (the individual *ME*). Of course, we have been trained in our generation to be egocentric, through the media, society, and our relationships. This mentality is reinforced and promoted everywhere we turn. But is it serving us? Fundamentally, we need the WE—other people, communities, and alliances—to support us in our growth, and to offer us the opportunity to support others.

The WE that I am referring to is not the obligatory conference that we attend annually where we meet with our own tribe: say, our insurance brothers and sisters that we see once a year. I'm talking about connecting with new tribes that we can feed and that can feed us, finding or creating the spaces where we can fuel one another's enthusiasm, giving and receiving new information

The reality is, we need to serve both the *I* and the *WE*. We serve the *I* when we place ourselves in situations that force us to grow. We serve the *WE* when we view life from other people's perspectives, step into other people's shoes, and learn to be more compassionate human beings. By flexing theses muscles, we get closer to becoming the shining diamond we have been placed on this earth to become.

DIVERSITY IS OPPORTUNITY

George Clooney, actor, director, producer, and one of my favorite people in the film industry, was on *Oprah* not too long ago. Toward the end of the show, Oprah asked George the following question: "If you could invite anyone in the world to a dinner party, who would you invite?"

Without much deliberation, George named the following people: President Clinton, Oprah (she giggled), film director Mike Nichols, his wife, television journalist Diane Sawyer, CNN news correspondent Christiane Amanpour, singer Tony Bennett, and architect Frank Gehry. "Why these folks?" Oprah asked George. He replied, "Because they are extremely bright and gifted people. They all come from different worlds. They would take me out of my world and educate me about theirs. That interests me." [6]

Sameness is a death knell to our brains. Meeting new people, reaching out to others, and getting involved in other people's worlds can become the catalyst for new perceptions and a whole new perspective on life. When we move out of our comfort zones, open up to new possibilities, our lives and our businesses stay fresh. They keep their sparkle, and we keep moving toward our highest aspirations.

Moving Beyond Our Comfort Zones is the fourth step in the initiation process. Here, we have learned the importance of agility and the ability to become free in our spirit. We appreciate the need to walk in someone else's shoes, to perturbate the system, and become a positive deviant. Without these understandings, we would not be prepared to share the Power of Our Story—the next stage in our unfolding.

For Further Contemplation

1. If you were free from fear, what changes would you make in your life?

2. Are there aspects of yourself or your business where you notice narrow-mindedness or shortsightedness?

3. Can you pinpoint where and why those aspects exist?

4. What changes can you make in your business that will move you away from those limited applications?

5. Is there anywhere in your business where you feel stuck? What actions can you take to get unstuck?

6. What actions could you take to become more of a positive deviant? More compassionate?

7. If you could invite anyone to a dinner party, whom would you invite? Why?

CHAPTER 6

THE POWER OF OUR STORY

> What makes this act so powerful—for both the teller
> and the listener—is that we meet in the moment of the story
> and emerge acknowledging our kinship with all of Life.
> Story reminds us that we are One.
>
> — Deborah Blanche, storyteller

Don't you just love a good story? As a child, do you remember jumping into bed early so that you could hear that fairytale that ushered you into dreamland? How about a funny joke or a movie that makes you laugh so hard your belly aches? Great stories stimulate the imagination. They allow the mind to explore new worlds, and arouse unexpected emotions. They remove us from our own everyday dramas: those dramas we want to break away from, even temporarily, to gain a different perspective.

Regardless of whether the story is sad or delightful, the tales that take hold of our hearts and leave indelible memories, furrow into the cells of our bodies, and alter our lives are the ones that have spiritual undertones. Think of those movies that you have had a personal, emotional connection to. Have they not changed your life, or your perspective on life, in some way?

Ray Bradbury's *Fahrenheit 451*, for instance, was a story that had a profound impact on my life. The idea that a government could demand that all books be burned, forbidding people to learn or imagine, frightened me so much in my youth that it made me wary of government controls. *Harold and Maude* changed my entire outlook on dying. Not only did Maude, a crazy old lady, and Harold, a demented young boy, enjoy meeting at funerals, they saw death from a completely different point of view than I ever had. No longer was death the morbid, end-of-existence model that I had grown up thinking it to be. Through these characters I learned to understand death as a celebration, a transitional journey for the soul, and a new beginning. *Apocalypse Now*, directed by Francis Ford Coppola, showed me war like I'd never seen it before, and brought home the frailty of life when pressed to its limits.

This is the power of story.

The Essence of Our Story

The "story" about our business needs to carry the same weight, create the same impact. Our story doesn't have to be about life and death, per se, but it must contain a personal, emotional connection for those we want to attract and engage.

There are seven elements that make up a good business story:

1. It starts with a good idea, or a problem that needs to be solved, or both. An example: identifying a segment of an industry that needs to be filled or diversified.

2. It has a protagonist who has the passion to want to solve the problem.

3. He or she must find creative ways to resolve the problem.

4. The story must have broad appeal.

5. There must be a personal and emotional connection to the audience one wants to attract.

6. The story should have a strong beginning, middle, and end.

7. There should be an unexpected twist or surprise.

Think about businesses you have heard of. What was it about their stories that moved you? What caught your attention and made you sit up and want to learn more? What propelled you to go to their website to read more about them? Was it the uniqueness of their business, the complexity or simplicity with which the business operated? Was it their marketing approach, or their clearly defined social concerns?

Now think about your own story. What is it that you want people to experience when they hear about your business? What are the feelings you want to evoke? Do you want them to have a good laugh from your wonderful idea? Do you want them to find profound meaning in your offering? Do you want them to be so excited, they will want to participate in some way?

Now, what is the story you want *other people* to share about your business? *This story* is more important than the story *we* share about *our* own business. This is where the "word of mouth" phenomena begins.

The stories that follow depict businesses that have left indelible marks in my mind and in the minds of thousands of others. Why, you may ask? Because of the "short story," "the buzz" that has spread about these businesses. While you read them, see how your business measures up in terms of content, originality, and authenticity.

In each case I provide the *short story*, the story that people are spreading about the business, and then I share the background story.

How the business began, how it grew; how each story incorporates the seven elements of effective storytelling to achieve the success the business now enjoys.

REMEMBER THE PET ROCK?

To this day, the story of the Pet Rock is one of my favorite business stories. Did you ever hear about it? The Pet Rock was created in the seventies. This little story made millions of people bellyache with laughter and inspired entrepreneurs worldwide to have the courage to carry out their own wacky ideas. It also made the creator, Gary Dahl, a fortune.

The "word of mouth" story that spread about the Pet Rock went something like this:

There is this rock for $3.95. What a joke! It's just a rock, but people are buying this thing like hotcakes!

The behind-the-scenes story goes like this:

Gary Dahl, the inventor, was a California advertising executive who, out having drinks with his buddies at a local bar one night, began a conversation about pets. Mr. Dahl informed his friends that he considered dogs, cats, birds, and fish to be a pain in the neck. "They make a mess," he said, "they misbehave, and they cost way too much money to maintain." He started bragging about his new pet—a pet that needed no maintenance, was extremely cheap and obedient, and had a great personality. It was his pet rock.

I am not sure if he actually owned this pet rock at the time, or if he was just teasing his buddies. In either case, his friends thought it was an off-the-wall idea and pretty soon they were tossing around all the things a pet rock would be good for.

Dahl spent the next two weeks writing the *Pet Rock Training Manual*, a step-by-step guide to having a happy relationship with your geological pet, including instructions on how to make it roll over and play dead, and how to house-train it.

"Place it on some old newspapers. The rock will never know what the paper is for and will require no further instruction." [1]

He packed the stone in a gift box shaped like a pet carrier, accompanied by the instruction book.

The Pet Rock was introduced at a major gift show in San Francisco and was an immediate hit. Neiman-Marcus pleaded for five hundred on the first order. *Newsweek* did a half-page story about the nutty notion, and by the end of the year, Gary Dahl was shipping thousands of Pet Rocks to people around the world. After appearing on *The Tonight Show*, twice, Mr. Dahl had become an instant millionaire.

For the thousands of people who were allergic to animals, or who could not afford a pet or own a pet because of apartment regulations, the Pet Rock was the perfect answer to their prayers.

Do you think this idea had an emotional connection to people? It absolutely did!

THE GREYSTON FOUNDATION

The short story that traveled about the Greyston Foundation went this way:

There is this amazing bakery in Yonkers. A lot of the employees used to be homeless and out of work. The company gives them housing, training, and rehabilitation. And on top of that, the bakery items are selling internationally.

The behind-the-scenes story goes like this:

In 1982, Roshi Bernie Glassman, an American Buddhist and social activist, opened a bakery in Yonkers, New York, to employ his Buddhist students. At the same time, he noticed the need to serve the underprivileged, the homeless, and the unemployed in the poverty-stricken area where he set up the bakery. Drawing on his years of Buddhist practice and compassion, Glassman established the Greyston Foundation.

Greyston Foundation's mission was and still is to support individuals and families as they forge a path to self-sufficiency and community transformation. By training men and women to cook, organize, and manage a business, Glassman taught them self-sufficiency, pride, and social responsibility. As Glassman helped people transform their lives, they, in turn, transformed the lives of others. The bakery is now a role model for companies wanting to inject social action into their business. Their axiom is: Greyston Bakery doesn't hire people to make brownies; they make brownies in order to hire people.[2]

Although Greyston started as a bakery, this entrepreneurial and spiritually grounded organization now operates an integrated network of not-for-profit and for-profit companies, providing jobs, workforce development, housing, youth services, and health care.

THE SWITCH TOWN

The short story that spread about the Switch Town went something like this:

I just came back from the weirdest family vacation in my life. We had fun, and learned a lot, but it was really spooky!

The behind-the-scenes story goes like this:

A small city north of Boston transformed their self-presentation from one of hangdog shame about the most unspeakable acts of prejudice in U.S. history to one of creativity as a New England landmark tourist spot. I am referring to the city of Salem, where, in 1692, a seven-month episode of hysteria led to imprisonment, torture, and twenty-five deaths. Women and men alike were charged with witchcraft, put in prison, and hanged. When the commonwealth government finally woke up to the plight of the victims, it was too late. Many had already died.[3]

After three-plus centuries of notoriety as the incarnation of prejudice, superstition, ill will, and bigotry masquerading as religious fervor, Salem, Massachusetts changed its "story."

Unable to ignore their horrific history, the residents of Salem made a decision to embrace the reality of what had occurred in their city, heal their wounds, and start fresh. They accomplished this with a two-pronged approach to a history they could never change. They created a historical museum that unflinchingly portrayed the realities of what had occurred. And outside the museum, all around the town, they developed a sense of humor in their self-image.

They started by naming the high-school sports team the Witches. Then, the *Salem Evening News* logo became the silhouette of a sorceress. Dramatizations of the infamous Salem witch trials are now a must-see for groups traveling through the area. Salem is noted for having some of the best Halloween parties anywhere, bar none. And if you keep your eyes open driving toward the legendary city, you can see on a passing billboard the words "Stop by for a spell." It is apparently their favorite slogan.

My first response to this humorous, even cutesy approach was to be appalled. Beyond that initial reaction, though, with empathy for the people of Salem, I could certainly feel their need to go on living, to create an environment for their children that did more than tie them to a burden from the past. The transformation that occurred in that city can actually be experienced as something inspirational.

JUST COFFEE

The short story that spread about Just Coffee went like this:

There is a coffee cooperative in Chiapas, Mexico, where the people can finally earn enough money selling coffee to stay in their village. They no longer have to break up their families by sending their husbands and teenage boys to the U.S. to earn a living. They can stay together and earn money in Mexico.

The behind-the-scenes story goes like this:

Eduardo Perez Derdugo, like hundreds of Mexicans looking for work to support their families, traveled through the desert on foot from Chiapas to Arizona. By the time he arrived in Arizona, he had been beaten and kicked by vigilantes. He was starving and close to death. The first words out of Eduardo's mouth were not "I need water! I am hungry!" but "To leave our land is to suffer." [4]

Tommy, a burned-out American hippie recently turned industrialist, met Eduardo just before Eduardo was deported. Eduardo explained to Tommy that he was a coffee grower from Salvador Urbina, a small town in Chiapas, but because coffee prices had reached an all-time low, farmers were forced to leave their land to make a living for their families.

Eduardo's story motivated Tommy to look for more support. He found three friends who all had one goal in mind: Let's find a solution to the border migration crisis.

Tommy and two friends drove to meet the growers from Salvador Urbina, to introduce the idea of starting a coffee cooperative.

When they reached the town, they saw that it was dying. Many of the young men had left their families to try to get to the U.S. There was no telephone service, no strong academic facility. The children had no shoes and could not afford books.

Tommy set up a meeting with the growers. And that day, the Just Coffee Cooperative was formed.

Using simple technologies that reversed the traditional business models of exploitation, twenty-two families got to work, pooling their talents. They learned about consensus decision making, Internet marketing, strategic planning, and the fine points of working in a multicultural environment.

There are now thirty-six families in the Just Coffee Co-op. From their initial earnings of 40 cents per pound, Just Coffee now pays $1.33 a pound—right to the grower. Now there are no "coyotes," no middlemen taking cuts. The co-op distributes their coffee to churches, health-food stores, restaurants, coffee shops, and farmers' markets throughout the Southwest.

Salvador Urbina now has a functioning school. The children have new clothes, new shoes, and new books. All thirty-six families have health-care benefits. Houses are being built, stores are popping up, residents are returning home from the U.S., and fewer people are leaving. Just Coffee is in the process of replicating this model in other Mexican villages.[5]

So, think of the story that is being circulated about your business and make sure it resonates and is in alignment with the story you want people to be sharing.

At the same time, you will want to make sure that the name of your business depicts the story you want shared.

CHOOSING THE RIGHT NAME

I'm sure there were times when you heard the name of a business and forgot it five minutes later. Or you heard the name of a company but the name didn't match the service or product, let alone make a lasting impression. Maybe the name of the business didn't stick because it was too long, too complicated, or you couldn't pronounce it. If the name of your business does not connect with your product or service, if it's not easy to remember, if it doesn't resonate with the story you want to share, the name will not be remembered. It's that simple.

I have read hundreds of books and seen thousands of movies, all because of their titles. I went to see the movies *Crash*, *The Hours*, *Cat on a Hot Tin Roof*, and *Eyes Wide Shut* because of their titles. I was drawn to read *To Kill a Mockingbird*, *The Knee of Listening*, *Eat, Pray, Love*, and the *I Ching*, because of their titles.

Books become bestsellers, films become blockbusters, and businesses thrive because their title has stimulated a reaction in the their audience. The name of your business plays a powerful role. It is a significant part of solidifying and spreading your brand.

Many business owners have used metaphors for their name; these can evoke a sense of complexity and solidity. The name *Oracle*, for instance, a massive Internet database created by Larry Ellison, suggests this kind of depth. When you hear the name *Oracle*, does it not imply a kind of history and knowledge? It conjures up images of Socrates, wise words to Alexander the Great from the priest of an ancient Egyptian shrine, or the Delphic Oracle of Greece. As a name, *Oracle* is uncomplicated. It's easy to read, easy to say, and quite memorable.

What about the name *Virgin*? Do we agree this name conjures up all kinds of images? Originally a British recording label, the Virgin brand has now branched out into Virgin Airlines, Virgin Vacations, Virgin Limousines, Virgin Games, and Virgin Galactic, privately built spaceships that provide tours in space. Why does this name have so much appeal? It brings forth thoughts of freshness, purity, something new, an idea whose time has come. I'm sure you can think of other reasons why this name is so powerful.

Here's another great name: *Yahoo!* Yahoo! screams for our attention: Listen to me! Look at me! And we do just that. For millions of people around the world, Yahoo! calls for our consideration. And we have certainly answered that call, by using their service a million times over.

VIAGRA

Here's another one of my favorite stories. I met the woman responsible for naming the drug Viagra. We met at a book party one night in New York City. I followed her around the room until there was a pause in one of her conversations. And then, I asked her if she could sit down and share with me how the name *Viagra* came to be. Since I had always been fascinated with titles and their significance to a business, I was most eager to listen.

We sat down and the woman leaned toward me and shared her tale. She told me that she had gathered together hundreds of men and women from across the U.S., from all kinds of backgrounds. For months on end, they wrote on large sheets of paper pinned on corkboards, mind mapping word after word until finally they narrowed the selection down to four words. These words created three images that they felt depicted the quality and essence of the drug—now the largest-selling sex drug on the market. Can you guess what those four words were?

They were *vivacious, water, Niagara Falls*—VIAGRA. Pretty cool, eh? I think the name worked.

What's in a Name?

Jay Jurisich, creative director and cofounder of Igor International, a naming and branding company based in San Francisco, says that a name can make or break a business. Picking a name is a process one should not take lightly: "The best product and company names require the least amount of advertising, as they are advertisements in and of themselves." He goes on to say, "A great name will differentiate you from competitors, and help you build a brand that ignites the passions of your customers. The name of your business should find a way into the hearts and minds of your customers, redefine and own the conversation in your industry, and engage people on as many levels as possible. The best names represent the ultimate process of boiling these ideas down into a word or two." [6]

Many times, the most memorable names are the ones that have depth. They don't reveal all they have to offer all at once, but keep surprising you with new ideas.

Jay offers a few tips on ways to reach your ideal name: Keep it objective. Does it have emotional kick? What does it look like, visually? How does it sound? And even: How does it taste?

THE EVALUATION PROCESS

When considering potential names for a business, it is vital that the process be kept as objective as possible. In other words, subjective personal responses to names, such as "I like it," or "I don't like it," or "I don't like it because it reminds me of my mother-in-law," have no bearing on whether or not a potential name will actually work in the marketplace as a powerful brand. In fact, the stronger the emotion connected with the name, in many cases, the better the reason to use it. Remember this while you discuss names with your board members or partners. If the conversation starts to heat up while discussing a name, you may want to pay close attention.

You will also want to think about the visual appearance of the name. How does it look on the page? How will it look on a poster, a billboard, or a TV ad? Is it simple, or complicated to read?

How does it sound? What happens to the mouth when you say it? How will it sound when it gets announced on radio and TV? Most importantly, how will it sound when your potential customer speaks it?

Let's take the name *Zoom*, and imagine that Zoom is a new soft drink. *Zoom* has a look, a feel, and a sound that conveys a certain spirit. It evokes speed, so we might imagine that it has a high sugar or caffeine content. It's probably bubbly, maybe tangy, and comes in a range of flavors. We definitely get a sense about the drink that will either propel us to purchase it or not. When we are naming a product, we clearly want to utilize and stimulate as many of the senses as possible.

A few more questions to ask yourself: Is the name distinctive? Can the name carry an ad campaign on its shoulders? Is it a force to be reckoned with? How relevant is the name to the positioning of the product or company? How will it affect the service being offered, or the industry being served? How many significant messages does the name "map" to? Answering all of these questions will help to evaluate the energy of the name, and its potency in the marketplace.

You may also want to list all the negative connotations and interpretations you can. If it's an innovative product, take the extra time to research the way its name translates in some large key population zones, like India and China. You would not want to offend someone from another culture by selecting a name that may be insulting to them. This may sound overly dramatic, but if you do not understand the significance of names in the Chinese context, you may end up with a story like Coca-Cola's. As it turns out, *Coca-Cola* in Chinese literally means "bite the wax tadpole." Not quite the image Coca-Cola desired for the Asian market.

As an embodiment of the brand's culture, values, personality and vision, a brand name needs to be free of negative connotations, and not to be confused with existing names. In a context like China, with a language that works by nuance and association, each written character is carefully chosen to bring across a suggestion or association to a very precise degree. Every name has a distinct flavor and impact.

In these days of growing globalization, extra consideration and care needs to be given when crossing cultural frontiers with your name or your brand.[7]

The Power of Your Story
and the Power of Your Name

There are millions of great stories. The stories I shared earlier in the chapter illustrate the throb, the pulse and the intention the creators initially had that brought their business to life. And their stories spread. Not because they spent thousands of dollars on advertising and promotion (although they may have), but because their stories contain the seven essential ingredients: passion; a problem; solving the problem; broad appeal; a personal, emotional connection; a beginning, middle, and end; and an unexpected twist. They have also uplifted the human spirit. And when you uplift the human spirit, there is no better story than that.

When the name of your business and your story merge; when you have fleshed out the who, what, where, why, and when; when you know at the core of your being that your story is meaningful, that it will benefit people, that your business is the absolute pinnacle of what you can offer; then you can feel secure, and rest in the knowledge that your business will take root and flower.

With attentive watering and nurturing, your flowers will grow, your garden will flourish, and you will be ready to move into the next phase of the initiation process: bringing your story to life—through the power of Ritual and Ceremony.

FOR FURTHER CONTEMPLATION

1. What story have you heard recently about someone's business that got you excited?

2. What did you love about the story?

3. Was there anything that you disliked about their story? What does this suggest to you in telling your own story?

4. What is the essence of *your* story?

5. What's the story you want other people to share about your business?

6. Does the name of your business truly reflect the story of your business? If not, can you brainstorm possibilities with greater resonance?

7. Are people familiar with your name? Your image? Your brand? What actions can you take to strengthen the brand, your name, and the significance of your story?

CHAPTER 7

RITUAL AND CEREMONY

I loved the atmosphere of the dance studio—
the wooden floor, the big mirror, everyone dressed in pink
or black tights, the musicians accompanying us—
and the feeling of ritual the classes had.

— Suzanne Vega, singer-songwriter

Since the beginning of civilization, humankind has hungered for ritual and ceremony. The sanctity that emerges from these practices connects us with the highest expression of ourselves and creates a feeling of belonging. Rituals that uplift the spirit provide us with a sense of wholeness. Just as nature provides us balance and order, the quality inherent in ceremony brings substance and joy into our lives.

Usually we associate ceremony and ritual with a religious act or consecration: the bar mitzvah honoring the male adolescent passage into adulthood in the Jewish tradition, the baptizing of a newborn child in Christianity, or the bowing down toward the direction of the holy city or kneeling before the altar in the Islamic and Hindu religions.

There are other rituals, like reading bedtime stories to our children, writing in our diaries, or gardening. These rituals, as common as they may seem, shape our lives and create a sense of calm, particularly during times of chaos and uncertainty when we yearn for stability. There are rituals that bring us tranquility and regularity. For instance, when I get up in the early hours of the morning, unplug the phone, meditate and write, this ritual makes me feel as if I am in a womb, secluded from the outside world. The peace I feel in this space helps me to access information from the purest place.

RITUAL AND OUR SENSES

I have always been fascinated by the nature and power of rituals: why they exist, why we choose one over another, why we derive so much pleasure participating in them. Quite simply, they give us solace, they make us *feel* good, they bring people of like minds together, they open us up to deeper, more expansive dimensions of ourselves and of life. Stemming from our primal need to connect with something greater, more significant than our limited self, rituals raise us into higher states of consciousness and captivate the present moment in ways that cannot compare with anything else we do.

We may ask, is it the rituals themselves that move us, or the feeling behind the rituals? We certainly *know* when these feelings of love, fullness, and rapture are present and when they are not. Have you ever received a massage where the therapist had the most sensitive touch and your body felt like it was melting as they massaged you? Have you had a massage where the therapist was mechanical? They were moving their hands around the right places, with the exact amount of pressure, but there was no love coming through their hands. What about when you get your hair cut, or when you buy a car, or purchase a home? The people helping you will either demonstrate true concern and care when they work with you or they will be just doing their job for the money or other motives.

We can all tell the difference. So, it's not the act itself, but the sacred element, the love, the attention and intention, the sense of wholeness behind the action that matters most. It's the *feeling* beneath the surface that we resonate with. This is true ritual.

WE ALL WANT TO BE MOVED

The seminars, lectures, and performances I have attended that cling to my memory are the ones that contain this soulful resonance. They have touched my heart, elevated my spirit, and helped me walk away feeling fuller and richer than when I'd walked in. When someone's presentation connects me to this deeper part of myself, I feel more alive, more expansive. I am appreciative and hopeful. Why hopeful? Because the presenter has connected me to myself, to the collective consciousness, and satisfied a spiritual hunger. And he or she has given me hope that there are more presenters out there offering the same experience to others.

Isn't this what we want to accomplish when we present? Don't we want to move people in a way where they are inspired, and want to learn more? Where they are motivated to ask us for our card and our website address? I am not suggesting that we create a religious experience per se, but that we communicate our message in a way that unites us more intimately with our audience. Deepak Chopra said in a YouTube video, "The stronger the ritual, the more powerful the experience. Ritual creates a *morphogenesis: morph*, meaning to shape, *genesis*, meaning to give birth. In other words, when we experience a powerful ritual, we experience transformation." [1]

What Kind of Presenter Are You?

I have listened to and watched hundreds of performers and presenters throughout the years, and the way each of them presents their material is as unique as the cells in their bodies. There are presenters who stand in front of the room barricaded behind a podium and, in a sense, hide their true essence. Then there are those who do their dog-and-pony show, speak in a monotone pitch, and use few, if any, imaginative stories. Too many times I am bored to tears and have walked away feeling ripped off, not only for the price of a ticket, but energetically.

And then there are presenters who engage and embrace their audience. They activate our senses through their enthusiasm, their honesty, and their passion. Because of their fearlessness to stand metaphorically naked, they pull us into their worlds, energizing us to be more, feel more. Even if we've walked into their presentation feeling agitated or depressed, within minutes we are transformed—not because they've used stimulating visuals or cool electronic props, but because of who they are and the sacredness they feel for themselves and their material.

When the Essential Is Missing

What happens when the sacred dimension of ritual and ceremony is missing from a presentation? What happens when an audience's senses and emotions are not engaged?

To illustrate what I mean, here are three stories from lectures or workshops I have witnessed. These brilliant authors, who have contributed much to the world with their magnificent discoveries, were unable to convey, at least on the day I saw them, the essential underlying element.

The Botanist

A renowned botanist and the author of many books on herbal alternatives was invited to speak to members of Congress in Washington, D.C., regarding the potency of organic herbs and their cost-effectiveness. The botanist was an articulate speaker and brought up several interesting arguments. He spoke about the difference between pharmaceutical drugs and herbal alternatives, the drug industry versus his own herbal botanicals. He pointed out the outrageous cost of drugs today and how the elderly, who need medicines the most, cannot afford to purchase them. He went on to speak about why herbal alternatives were more "user friendly," less expensive, nonaddictive, and less invasive than traditional allopathic medicine.

And he told us about all the herbs that he personally grows in his fifty-acre garden—but he didn't *show* us. He didn't take us on a tour of his garden or display the plants for us to touch and see. A few plants sitting on the table in front of him would have added so much more depth to his presentation and created a palpable visual for the audience.

By *showing* Congress, not just *telling* them, by being more animated, more passionate, he might have knocked these Congressmen and Congresswomen right off their wooden chairs. And the bill he wanted to pass would have received more votes.

The New Age Speaker

A well-known author and speaker in the New Age community gave a talk at a conference I attended. I was really looking forward to hearing this man speak, because I had read many of his books and totally loved his message. As he spoke, he showed us beautiful slides of nature and sacred sites from around the world. They were colorful and intriguing, but I had seen many of them before in *National Geographic* magazines. He kept showing slide after slide, reeling off quotes by other authors and poets. He used only a few of his own words. After the talk, I sat there, stunned. Here I had listened to this internationally known speaker and author, but felt like I had never heard *him*. All I remember about his talk were the beautiful images.

Technology can be a useful tool when it adds emphasis and dimension to our content. But it can never replace the human element, the sacred power of the heart.

And then there are speakers who go on and on, as if they were delivering a soliloquy. They take no breath, no pause, and do not consider the overall needs of the audience. Like Sam, my next example.

No Pause for Integration

Sam is a successful businessman and holds seminars regularly. Sam is a bright light in the business world. He shares intriguing approaches to business theory, provides great wisdom from the masters, and has great stories to tell. However, the way he presents is like a machine gun—shooting out bullets of information at lightning speed for four days and three nights, nonstop. He leaves no time for bodies and brains to assimilate all the brilliant ideas he's tossing out.

After one of his workshops, I contacted a few of the women who had attended, and it was unanimous: all six of us had become ill when we returned home. The men I spoke to were also exhausted, but had bounced back to life after a day of rest. I found these responses not only interesting, but disheartening. And then I took some time to think about them.

Women in general process information differently from men. The way women integrate information seems to be more assimilative, contextual, and multisensory. And as we all age, men and women alike, we shift from the tendency to wolf down and memorize huge chunks of "facts" to a more ruminative approach. We handle material with more subtlety and sophistication; we integrate all the materials we're working with from multiple levels of awareness simultaneously.

This type of learning is often more "embodied," drawing on a broader range of physiological responses and learning modalities from our physical instrument. It brings in every sensory system, and incorporates learning into every cell of the body. It's a form of learning that has often gone by the name of *wisdom*.

The machine-gun type of teaching format has been around for some time, used in situations we typically think of as "masculine"—Army boot camp, for instance, or med school—and in situations that typically address adolescent or young-adult learners. The instructors, usually men, think that if they break down their audience physically, mentally, and emotionally, participants will absorb the information faster. This forced approach to learning is a military model that shows complete disregard for humans, and personally, I find it abusive. There are a variety of learning modalities, and we need to respect the variation. We also need to bring in the love, the care for pacing, the tailoring of the process to the needs of the learner, and the conscious awareness of ritual and ceremony.

There are many ways to honor the body-mind instrument. Instructors can offer meditation sessions during their course, introduce hatha-yoga stretches, build in more breaks, and program in hands-on exercises and periods for reflective assimilation alternating with interactive group communication, so participants can talk about the material they've just heard to know what the brain has received.

When speakers start pacing themselves in a way that allows every member of their audience to breathe into the information so that it gets integrated into the mind, body, and spirit of each person, we will all feel better about attending these informative seminars. And we'll all get more out of them.

Presentations with Soul

Now let's look at some stories that exemplify the love, the care, and the inherent qualities of ritual and ceremony that we want to bring forth when we speak or make a presentation.

The Architect

Bruce Coldham is a green architect living in New England, currently with the firm Coldham and Hartman. Several years ago, I represented Bruce and suggested he present a program entitled "The Value of Design" to local homeowners, demystifying the myths and misconceptions about the architect's profession. At that time, Bruce rarely made public appearances, and when he did, he would freeze. We worked together on developing his performance skills and it didn't take long for him to loosen up and feel at ease in front of people.

We looked all over the Amherst-Northampton area for the perfect place to hold Bruce's event and finally decided on the Lord Jeffrey Inn, a lovely historic venue in Amherst, Massachusetts.

The ambience of the garden room where the event was held was ideal. It overlooked tropical plants and a cascading waterfall. People could walk around the patio, sit and chat, meet and greet one another without pressure. We brought in delicious hors d'oeuvres to set in motion the audience's taste buds. Scented and textured materials were displayed for the audience to touch and smell. Bruce set up his computer to show "before and after" renovations of residential and commercial buildings, and how adding a few extra feet to a room or a home would dramatically change the entire structure. We covered the walls with enlarged photos of his designs to display his versatility and make participants feel confident in Bruce's ability.[2]

But the most impressive part of the evening was Bruce himself. He was personable without being pushy. He was enthusiastic, without being overbearing. He delivered his talk in a way that revealed his love for architecture and design, and allowed time for people to assimilate the information. He made everyone feel comfortable, informed, up-to-date with the newest and most expeditious ways to save money while expanding their homes and beautifying their spaces. He never tried to "sell" his service. He educated his audience, answering questions during and after the event. His relaxed, kinesthetic approach activated people's senses, and satisfied their hunger—on all levels. His talk was so successful that Bruce called me a few days later to tell me that several people had called him wanting estimates for the expansion of their homes.

THE SINGER

Lila Downs is the Mexican-American singer whose debut song, "Burn It Blue" from the award-winning film *Frida*, placed Lila in international circles. The first time I saw Lila perform was at the Lensic Performing Arts Center in Santa Fe, New Mexico. All 850 seats were filled. But let me tell you, no one was sitting for long; we were propelled up off our seats to participate in one of the most enthralling musical performances I've ever experienced. I've never seen anyone put so much heart and soul into a musical performance; Lila lost herself in the music, *became* the characters in her stories, and merged with the audience, all at the same time. She used huge video images to enhance each song, while she leapt and danced from one end of the stage to the other. Bodies were bopping up and down in every seat, the balcony was filled with ecstatic dancing silhouettes, and people were boogying onto the stage.

When the audience left the theater that night, they streamed out still singing and dancing into the parking lot. I looked around to see the expression on people's faces. Every face was glowing, smiling. We had all been engaged in a highly charged, ecstatic ritual, and one we will most likely never forget.

The Presence

We don't need cutting-edge technology or exuberant voices accompanied by video images to create a soulful experience. We can be moved when someone is simply *being present*. Few people have this skill. But when they do, everyone around them experiences morphogenesis, the birth of a new form, a new way of being. Dr. Richard Moss, international speaker and teacher of contemporary psychology, creates this transformation every time he speaks.

I had never heard of Dr. Moss before watching a video of him. And although video is a rather flat medium, through which one is not apt to experience a visceral response, I did have such a reaction. Which was why I signed up to see him when I heard he was going to speak at a nearby conference.

Sitting ten feet away from Dr. Moss was indeed more powerful than watching him on video. And as I watched him, he became the embodiment of his talk: *Presence is the turn-on!* Sharing his experiences, his wisdom, his delight with the challenge of living in the world, he exemplified the importance of owning one's presence without pretense. He was the personification of understanding himself to be enough. He was totally present and in the moment. There was no need for notes or slides, music or technology. There were no bells and whistles. He *was* the bells and whistles. He was the color, the music, and the technology. His fullness moved everyone in the room to tears. We realized, that day, that we could be who we were without airs, without masks, and still be superbly effective.

His presentation and the passion that emanated from his being forever changed the way I present my material. He taught me a very important lesson that day: all the knowledge and information we consume is of nebulous value if we cannot *be*, in the moment, with others and ourselves.

Becoming Established in the Sacred Element

So . . . do we want our audience sitting in their seats yawning, looking out into space, putting on lipstick, or looking at their watches because they're bored? Do we want them to become ill because of a spitfire approach? Do we want to see them walking out of the room wondering why they had wasted their time and money to come see us? Heavens, no!

We want our listeners to be interested, captivated, intrigued. Our role is to be the channel for the information we want to convey. Nothing more. Nothing less. So, I beg you, give yourself permission to be naked, present, outrageous, funny, and loving when you stand before your audience. Reveal yourself in this way, and you will reveal your inner light. You will *become* the light. You will allow that sacred element within you to blaze forth and create that blessed bond with every person in front of you. Perhaps this is why Dr. Moss said, "Everything about my speaking changed when I fell more in love with my audience than with my material." [3]

When we as presenters bring these essential qualities to the forefront without holding back, we give our listeners the opportunity to connect with that same space within themselves. We honor their pace and their ability to learn, their own creativity and capacity for delight. They feel secure in our presence, and thereby safe to dream, to feel their aliveness, and to trust that they too can be who they are in the most fundamental way.

Ritual and Ceremony brings us to an apex in this book. It's a keystone arch for us. The steps we've come through have prepared us conceptually and philosophically to integrate the initial stages of the Science of Spiritual Marketing. The chapters that follow are of a more practical nature. They will help us to create more structure as we move into our marketing strategies—beginning with the next step: Mind Mapping.

For Further Contemplation

1. Make a list of the speakers and performers you admire. What is it about them that sparks your admiration?

2. What are some ways you can bring these qualities into your own presentations?

3. Does fear come up for you when you present? If so, how can you become free from this fear? What steps can you take to let yourself be more at ease with your audience?

4. Are you willing to share who you are with your audience? If not, what do you need to do to make this possible?

5. Is there a balance of engagement and release when you present? Do you offer enough stretch breaks and other opportunities for your audience to integrate information into their bodies?

6. Do you stimulate your audience kinesthetically? Are their senses being activated by your material?

7. Are there other ways you can bring the qualities of ritual and ceremony into your presentation?

CHAPTER 8

MIND MAPPING YOUR STRATEGY

How can we be sure to cover the micro and macro—
the small details, and the big picture? How can we
experience visual thinking, brainstorming, and identifying
relevant issues in a single glance? Mind mapping.

— Author unknown

Mind mapping is a technique of arranging ideas and their interconnections visually. It is a fascinating method that accelerated-learning advocates and progressive teachers have been using for years. What I love about mind mapping is its simple design and easy formula for learning, its versatility and ability to benefit the auditory, visual, oral, and kinesthetic learner. I don't know of a better way than mind mapping to absorb and remember information, brainstorm, be introduced to a subject, explore its parameters, and see the entire scope of a project or strategy in one fell swoop.

I was introduced to mind mapping twenty-five years ago during an accelerated-learning course in New York City. I remember sitting in the audience, so impressed with its brilliant simplicity that I leaned over to my friend and said, "Had I been shown this technique in high school, I would have passed all my classes with As."

Later that day, I realized how true that statement was. Especially when recalling my high-school history teacher! If only Mr. Newton had used mind mapping when he so boringly discussed the events that took place in U.S. history. You know, the ones we were supposed to remember for our tests, our midterms and our finals. To me, the dates and events seemed so unrelated, so isolated. Had he used mind mapping, I would have connected the dots, remembered the dates, and retained 100 percent of the information. Instead, I consistently got Cs in the subject.

Tony Buzan, author of *Mind Maps at Work*, says,

> A Mind Map is a powerful graphic tool, which provides a universal key to unlock the potential of the brain. It harnesses the full range of cortical skills—word, image, number, logic, rhythm, color, and spatial awareness—in a single, uniquely powerful manner. In so doing, it gives you the freedom to roam the infinite expanses of your brain. Mind Mapping can be applied to every aspect of life where improved learning and clearer thinking will enhance human performance.[1]

A mind map will:

- Give you an overview of a large subject or area.
- Enable you to plan and make choices, and let you know where you are going and where you have been.
- Encourage problem solving by showing you new creative pathways.
- Enable you to be extremely efficient.
- Be enjoyable to look at, read, muse over, and remember.

- Attract and hold your eye and brain.

- Let you see the whole picture and the details at the same time—in other words, help you connect the dots.

DESIGNING OUR MARKETING MIND MAP

By designing a mind map for your marketing strategy, you create a visible diagram that shows you all the pieces in one glance. It illustrates where you are in the present moment, and what still needs to be done. The more you revert to this map, the faster you can check off each section of your analysis and strategy and reach your goals.

The first step is to draw a circle in the center of a piece of paper. Imagine that you are drawing a sun; not too big—because you will want to extend lines out from this sun. In the center of the circle, write your name or the name of your business. The circle represents you, as you are the sun.

For the sake of this exercise, let's say you are a feng-shui consultant and the name of your business is *Internal Peace with Fran Drake*.

The second step is to draw, say, 8 to 12 lines radiating out from your central sun or circle. We will call these lines the rays of the sun, as these are the ways in which you will radiate, reach out to the world and spread your work.

On the first ray, write the word *WEBSITE*.

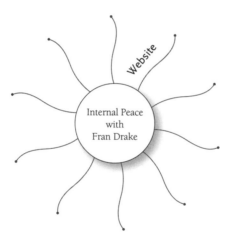

Now, on a separate piece of paper, write down all the aspects of your website that you want to include or address in designing it. If you already have a website, this may give you an opportunity to look at each aspect more closely.

We'll start with the *menu bar*. The menu bar categorizes your site. It helps your audience to navigate the site and allows them to see the different segments of your business and the opportunities that you offer. It gives them background information about your company and a tangible way to connect with your business.

The menu bar is also referred to as the *sidebar* or the *navigation bar*. Some sites position the bar or list of options across the top of their site, some on the side, some on both.

On a separate sheet of paper, flesh out your menu bar. The number and type of categories you list on this sheet will determine how many internal sublinks you want your audience to visit on your site. Just remember: less is more. Too much information on a site can confuse people and turn them off.

Here's a sample of menu-bar items from Fran's hypothetical feng-shui site.

THE MENU BAR

- *What Is Internal Peace?* Here you can describe what Internal Peace is about. You can place your mission statement here, or some history about the company.

- *About Fran:* This is where you include your photo and your bio.

- *Workshops and Presentations:* List the current types of workshops, talks, and presentations you are offering and define them in a few short, juicy paragraphs.

- *Upcoming Events:* List the who, what, where, and when of your upcoming workshops and other public apperances. You can also include sample flyers on this page.

- *Consultations:* This links to the webpage that communicates how you set up your consultations, what a consultation consists of, and the time it typically entails. Subheads may specify consultations for individuals and consultations for organizations, with a brief description of each.

- *Coaching:* If you offer coaching sessions, define how the coaching session is different from the consultation. Explain if your coaching sessions are conducted in person and/or by telephone.

- *Fran's Store:* Display visuals of books, CDs, and other materials, with a short description of each, and link to a subprogram for online purchasing.

- *Newsletter:* This could be a monthly or bimonthly online or hard-copy newsletter that you offer. People can sign up for the newsletter on your website. (More on newsletters in Chapter 13, Write to Learn.)

- *Media:* This is where you can present webcasts, podcasts, live audio broadcasts, or a video. You can also list articles you have written, interviews, or articles written about you.

- *Contact Fran:* This is where you place your e-mail address, your phone number, and any mailing address you want to make public. Many consultants have an automatic link from their website to their e-mail account.

After you have fleshed out the WEBSITE ray, think about including other rays that detail specific ways you can reach out to an ever-widening audience. For our friend Fran and her feng-shui consultantship, there are quite a few that come to mind.

Other Rays of Outreach

- *Brochure:* Since paper travels, and you too will be doing a lot of traveling, you will want to create a brochure that you can leave with people wherever you go. A brochure is much easier to write after your website has been completed. You've done most of the work by designing the website. Now it's a matter of extracting the pertinent information onto a few pages that are attractive and easy to read.

- *Intro programs:* On a separate sheet of paper, flesh out all the venues in your geographical area where you could offer an introductory program about feng shui. For instance, you could present an intro program to realtors, builders, architects, and interior designers. You could also arrange an intro at a local home-improvement store, or a bookstore, or a community-minded café.

- *Home presentations:* List all the people you know who have experienced your good work. They may want to invite friends over to hear about the benefits of incorporating feng shui into their home or office. The home presentation is one of the reasons Tupperware became a multimillion-dollar business. Not only do they have a great product that is now a household name, but they started introducing their products in the home. Why? Because people love to be in a relaxed environment, among friends, drinking tea or wine as they hear about ways to improve their lives.

- *Local networking groups, and civic or service organizations:* Look up and list local organizations that welcome speakers to present at their luncheons or meetings. These might include Rotary, Lions and Lionesses, and business groups.

- *Not-for-profit organizations:* Not-for-profits (NFPs) have fundraisers, which can offer a wonderful opportunity to introduce feng shui to an interesting and potentially interested audience. Consider offering a consultation as an item in their fundraiser auction—and think of the public notice when your name gets yelled out by the auctioneer in front of hundreds of people. NFPs may also hire speakers to present at their monthly meetings.

- *For-profit businesses:* Such businesses might include banks, law firms, local insurance agencies or companies, music companies, and art galleries, as well as the local chamber of commerce.

- *Articles:* Write an article in a local, regional, or national newspaper having to do with building, architecture, and realty or home improvement. Write an article in a professional magazine with appeal to a specialty audience like chiropractic practitioners, physicians, naturopathic medicine, dental care, building and interior decorating, or computer design.

- *Conferences:* Many professions potentially interested in your expertise host conferences or professional-development symposia that meet monthly, quarterly, or annually. After searching out where these conferences are located, see about becoming a presenter.

- *Sponsors:* There is nothing better than finding a sponsor—an organization that is in alignment with your mission, that believes in your product or service and that is reputable and recognizable. They can add support to your cause in many ways. They can lend you their name, help offset advertising cost, or provide a space for you to present your material. A sponsor who also has a substantial audience can help facilitate "spreading the word" by notifying their audience about you and your services.

- *International networking organizations:* These include BNI (Business Networking International), Le Tip, Rotary, Business for Social Responsibility, and many others. Here too, you can Google international networking organizations and find hundreds. The purpose of these organizations is to support each member and to share interesting products or services, like yours, with people they meet.

Before you sign up for one of them, check out a range of these groups to see which ones you click with.

- *Media (TV, radio):* Google to find local, regional, and national media outlets. Every TV and radio show is listed on the Web. It's a matter of locating their contact information and finding out who their audience is, and feeling out if their audience would be interested in the information you want to provide.

As you start to flesh out your mind map, some of the rays or your ideas may be so big and broad they could feel overwhelming or intimidating. In that case, you can create a mind map for each specific idea or ray. In drawing your map, your business name does not necessarily have to be in the center of the map; it can be a starting point at the top or bottom, or at one side or the other of your expanse of paper. Once you get going, you will have so many ideas for each endeavor that you will want to create a map for each one. If you have multiple businesses, create a mind map for each business, and then a map for each ray.

The beauty of creating your mind-map template is that once you have fleshed out all the options for your business on a local level, you can easily generate another map for reaching out regionally, nationally, and even internationally.

THE BOTTOM LINE OF MAPPING

Mind mapping is the most creative tool I know for visualizing all the possibilities of whatever enterprise we want to explore. I use it all the time to look at a problem, or options, or just to see the places my imagination goes when I explore a new idea. I have met people in restaurants who share their business ideas with me. I immediately grab a napkin or a sheet of paper and start drawing a mind map, because it leaves everything and nothing to the imagination. The overview is stimulating and exciting, and one that can be navigated and charted during the course of our ever-expanding progress, whatever our profession or whatever the idea.

The more we flesh out each and every category in our map, the more we see the actual overabundance of places there are to network, bridge, and connect with people and organizations who may be interested in our products or services. I cannot begin to count the number of clients and workshop participants who have mind mapped their way to financial and personal success.

You can start by just using a pencil or crayons, or you can purchase a mind-mapping software program by Googling the words "mind-mapping software" and selecting the software that appeals to you the most. In the meantime, enjoy the discovery. Happy mapping!

As the eighth step in the initiation process, Mind Mapping stimulates the imagination, shows us all the possibilities inherent in our business and its relation to the world around us, and gives us a tangible picture of the strategy to move forward. Our motivation and our intentions are clear, and we are ready for the next step: Our Soulful Collateral.

 FOR FURTHER CONTEMPLATION

1. Begin thinking about a mind map of your own. What words can be placed in the center of your mind map? Is it the name of your business? Or a central concern you want to understand more clearly or brainstorm an approach to dealing with? Or a project you want to initiate?

2. What are the names of the rays that surround and radiate out from the center of your map? How can you flesh out each ray?

3. Do you need to do more research to fill in your rays? If so, where do you need to go? Who do you need to call?

4. Do you need to create additional mind maps for each ray? Do you need to map out how certain rays connect with each other?

5. Does your current website include all the information now listed on your new mind map? If not, perhaps it's time to update your site.

CHAPTER 9

OUR SOULFUL COLLATERAL

When we reach people at the core of their being
through our words, our images and our light,
our message will travel far beyond those we meet face to face.

— Author unknown

Our Soulful Collateral includes our hard-copy and online materials, such as our websites, cards, brochures, flyers, and ads. It also includes our live and taped presentations. These materials support us in establishing our personal and business identity, showcasing us to the world. Their function is to be our extended arms and legs, to touch our audience, cultivate interest, provide a platform for us to speak out and proudly voice: "Hey, look at me. Read this! My product, my service will change your life, it will make your life happier, healthier, wealthier, wiser . . . if you do."

Businesses go to great lengths, and tremendous expense, to make sure their materials are seen and heard—but through what means? We know that some marketing techniques do not work. And we know some can be actively harmful. Blasting our messages using high-voltage color, hammering our audience with loud noises, scrambling the senses with frenetic, crosscutting imagery, or using any harsh means is no longer acceptable. In this chapter and in this initiation process, we will focus on establishing more soulful ways to connect with those people we want to reach.

Before we begin, I'd like to point out that there is a sequence in which these marketing materials are to be created, and why.

The Biography Is First

Regardless of how many years you have been in business, or stayed at one job, the biography is the first piece of collateral to be written. In fact, I would suggest having this document up-to-date and ready to be printed out at a moment's notice. You never know when you will need it. The biography is not just a piece of paper that lists your current and previous jobs. It is a live document that can convey more than you realize.

The biography synthesizes who we are, what we have accomplished, what we are offering in the present, and what we intend to offer in the future. When we fuse our past, present, and future within this one document, we align with the internal energetic forces of our being; we recognize our power, stand in it, and comprehend our role in the universe in more intricate ways.

Carolyn Myss, author of *Energy Medicine* and world-renowned speaker on the subject of energy therapies, talks about this correlation in her CD *Personal Healing.* She says, "Your *biology* becomes your *biography.*" [1] In other words, our physical, biological makeup creates our present, and determines the way we play out our life. I would like to add to this by saying, "Your *biography* becomes your *biology.*" Because when we are in alignment with our soul's calling when have synthesized the past, present, and future of our work, when we have acknowledged all that we have accomplished and we see it in black and white, it changes the way we feel about ourselves. It transforms our inner dynamics, and our external energy field.

This not-so-subtle phenomenon has proven itself to me again and again. It's an amazing thing. When clients complete their biography, they begin to feel different. They resonate with a higher frequency. They stand taller. They're more self-assured. As they walk around with this new energetic alignment, they begin to realign with those people and opportunities they want to attract.

I didn't believe it myself, at first, and then it kept happening over and over.

For example: I was working with Susan, an acupuncturist in Santa Fe, New Mexico. Susan was an excellent D.O.M. (Doctor of Oriental Medicine), but she wasn't clear who her audience was. After her consultation, what surfaced was: her audience was clearly women undergoing a difficult transition through menopause. I started to help her write her biography. We were only halfway through when she started getting calls from women wanting to come see her. By the time her biography was done, she told me her clientele had doubled. She hadn't done any advertising, and yet she was attracting precisely those women she had understood to be her true audience.

Another woman called me and told me that after we'd worked on her bio, she landed the best account she'd ever had—and she got engaged.

I was astounded at how quickly these changes were happening. And then it dawned on me: Of course! It's perfect! Creating the biography aligns us, alchemically, with our innate focus. This realignment sets a direction and a magnetizing power. After writing our biography, everything else we write or present becomes easier, because we are aligned with the soul. We are in the energetic pattern and flow of our most powerful essence.

Now, can you imagine? If we experience this kind of transformation when we complete our biography, consider how we'll feel and how our business will expand when we align with our website.

The Website

The website is our global calling card. The minute people log on to our site, they experience a visceral response—it is immediate: they find themselves either confused or impressed, drawn in or turned off. Before they read a word on the home page, they experience an energetic reaction. That first impulse will determine whether they stay on or move to another site.

Even the way our website is navigated is vital. If there is too much information, if it looks too cluttered, or if the visitor can't travel through it easily, they will not hang around. If the menu bar or the e-commerce component is challenging to negotiate, people will not take the time to figure it out. Each page must be easy to read and use.

I'm sure you've seen sites that have multitudes of products to sell. Or there is so much information you hardly know where to start. Not to mention the neon lights and banners that lure you onto another site or into a blog, or a podcast or a webcast. And round and round you spin.

There are three things people look for when they search the Web and log on to a site. They want a pleasurable experience, quality information, and navigational simplicity. That's it.

Resonating with Your Site

As I mentioned earlier, there are many public-relations specialists and Web experts who are gifted writers and work with owners of small and large businesses to design and create marketing materials. I have met many of them throughout the years. Talented and creative as they are, few of them understand how to midwife information with a client. Instead, they project their thoughts and ideas onto a client, or write the text themselves, and wonder why the end result doesn't bring the fruits they had intended.

A gentleman who had taken one of my workshops several years ago contacted me after the course, telling me how much he loved my work, and asked if I would be interested in creating a more sophisticated website than the one I had. He was quite savvy in the area of Internet marketing and design and I thought, why not! I was in need of an upgrade, and the price was reasonable. So I agreed.

We spent the next several months transforming the site. We worked day and night. I pretty much gave my life to this project. Three months later, close to a nervous breakdown from the nonstop effort, we launched the site. The result was a disaster. The experience made me think of something a wise teacher once said: "We always know by the results if we've made the right decision." Well, the result of this effort was horrendous!

Usually when I send out my e-mail newsletter, I hear from people right away: new and past clients inquiring about consultations and upcoming workshops. After I sent out my newsletter announcing the new site, no one responded. Not one person. *Nada!* I was in total shock! The site was beautiful, elegant; it had all kinds of audio and video segments; but something was off. It wasn't my site. The material, the look, the feel did not represent what I was about. The energy resonating from the site had nothing to do with me; it was all about the consultant.

I immediately scratched the project, and started over. I worked meticulously for three weeks to get the site back to where I could feel good about every single word and image on every single page—where I could put my "Good Housekeeping" seal of approval on it. Minutes after sending out my NEW newsletter announcing my new site, I heard from over a hundred people. It was the most powerful lesson I had experienced to date on trusting the spiritual/holistic approach.

And 100-percent proof that there is an energetic response to our materials. If these materials do not come from that deep, authentic place within *us*, where *we* vibrate with every word and sentence and image we select, our materials will not be effective. We will not draw the audience we want to attract. This principle applies to every piece of marketing collateral we create, whether it's a brochure, an ad, or a flyer.

THE BROCHURE

Once the website is complete, it's much easier to create the brochure. You've already done most of the work. Now it's a matter of selecting the pertinent information that you expressed on your website and shrink-wrapping it, as I like to say, for the brochure.

The brochure is what you display and hand out when you make a presentation or attend a conference. Or you might meet someone while getting your car washed or waiting for your Chinese takeout meal. You never know! The brochure is a very important piece of your collateral. I would not skimp on it or take it lightly.

The information on your brochure should be spare, uncluttered, to the point, and a simple introduction to your work. Be careful not to use too many colors or words on one page. Allow the eyes to glide through the material so your reader enjoys "the read" and the look and feel of the brochure. If you decide to use photos, use them only if they enhance your message, and don't use too many. Work with a professional graphic designer to help you with the colors, the font choices, and the layout. If writing this document is challenging, work with a public-relations/marketing consultant who knows how to midwife the information with you and who can help edit the material as well.

THE ADVERTISEMENT

Even more than the brochure, the advertisement needs to be fine-tuned and shrink-wrapped to perfection. Because there is limited space, you will want to be extremely frugal and precise with the words and images you select. One ad, or a series of ads, can make a huge impact in drawing your audience to you.

To outline the essentials of advertising, I created a CD called *To Advertise or Not to Advertise, That Is the Question.* In it, I speak about when, and when not, to advertise. There are pointers on advertising an event, a display ad, targeting the ad, timing the ad, giving your readers a reason to act immediately, and much more. The point is: Take your time. Really think about the words you use and the impact they will have on your audience.

In my twenties, while living in New York City, I had a business called Professional Organizers, where I helped to organize people's moves. I decided to place an ad in *New York* magazine. I really had to think about the words for this ad, because the minimum cost was over $400.

I started from the awareness that most people, especially those living in Manhattan, are traumatized when it comes to moving. Once you find an apartment or a condo in Manhattan, you stay there for years, the rent stabilizes, and after ten, twenty, thirty years, you accumulate a lot of stuff.

Thinking about the emotional upset people experience when they move, I thought to counter their fear and turn it around. So I placed an ad that read, "Moving Can Be an Enjoyable Event. Call Professional Organizers! We'll make your move a breeze!" This little ad brought me three years of business.

Before Creating These Materials

Before creating the brochure, the flyer, the website, or the ad, there are questions to be asked and answered: Who is my audience? What are their concerns? What questions do they need answers to? What images should I use that will convey my message? Would a picture of a forest, or a picture of a beach, convey the feeling I want to express? Would children playing in a sandbox, or an elderly couple feeding ducks by a lake, be truer to the intention? Should I use a clean, sparse, sophisticated look or a calm, melodic look?

Whatever the hard-copy materials you are designing, these questions need to be asked. It's about thinking holistically about your business, and your audience. Seeing their needs and concerns, and then getting to the point—succinctly, using the least amount of words.

At the same time we are asking these questions about our audience, we are checking inside ourselves. We are getting very still, so we can listen. By asking these questions from this quiet, receptive place, we get the clarity we need; we become the channel for the wisdom that exists inside us.

When we ask from this reference point, our materials become an extension of who we are, and what we represent. We reveal the core purpose for our business. As a result, our audience knows within seconds if they want to work with us or not. There is no hesitation or doubt, because we have told the truth, the whole truth, and nothing but the truth.

How Do We Get to the Truth?

Here's an exercise that can support you in transferring your thoughts and ideas to any marketing material you want to create. I have chosen "the flyer" to illustrate the process.

Please get a notebook or writing pad and something to write with. Locate a space in your home where it is comfortable and quiet, where you can be alone and undisturbed.

You can sit on the floor or in a nice, comfy chair. Just be sure to have the notebook and pen in front of you or close by. Relax.

Take a deep breath and close your eyes. Let the breath out slowly.

Take another deep breath and let it out slowly.

When you are completely relaxed, contemplate the question: *What is it my audience wants to read and see on this flyer that will let them see if what I'm offering is for them? What will draw them to this event, to this workshop, or to this presentation?*

Keep asking until the information comes to you. When you hear specific words and phrases, write them down on your notepad.

Do not be concerned about the sequence of the words at this point. Just focus on the phrases, the tone, the feeling of the words, and on what your upcoming workshop or presentation is about. Keep asking yourself what your audience needs to read and see on this page for them to be clear about the nature and value of this upcoming event and be drawn to it.

Keep asking and keep writing until all the elements—who, what, when, and where—have been transcribed onto the page.

Now ask yourself: What image, if any, would your audience like to see on the flyer? Perhaps it is your logo, your photo, or both, or another image entirely, that evokes the essence of what you want to convey. If your event is located in an exotic, serene, or exciting location, you may want to display a picture of the place where it will be held.

Think about the colors. Do the colors on your flyer reflect the sentiment of the text, of your work? Will these colors resonate with your audience?

When all the text and all the accompanying images and colors are clear in your mind, you may want to seek out a graphic designer to help you create the template for your flyer. I suggest you use a professional, unless of course design is an area in which you are gifted.

OUR PERSONAL COLLATERAL

As important as it is to create our hard-copy materials, there is also the need to perfect or at least be comfortable with our on-screen, on-air, or in-person presentation. How we look and behave, as we share our message, is also part of our collateral. If we go into an interview with crooked glasses, with slacks that are too tight or too baggy, what is the message we are conveying? It may seem to the person we are meeting that we don't care. And they may think, *Well, if you don't care, why should I?*

How we present ourselves physically applies whether we are going on a job interview, meeting someone for the first time, or appearing on a show to be interviewed.

Before appearing on any TV or radio show, we need to have all our marketing materials complete. We've seen how the process of preparing them places us more in sync with our message. We feel more in our own skin, more confident. When our audience hears what we have to say, they will be more apt to go to our website or call us to learn more about our business.

So those hard-copy pieces of your collateral need to be ready before you appear on any show. Now, let's assume that you have completed these materials, and you've been asked to appear on a radio or TV talk show. Are you ready? Have you built your interview muscle?

THE INTERVIEW MUSCLE

Most of us have not built the "interview muscle." It's no one's fault. We simply have not worked with the media on a regular basis. We don't know the ways in which we need to be on point with our message so that all the pieces—how we look, sound, and articulate our message—are seamless and effortless.

It's not possible to be nervous and calm at the same time. It's not possible to be preoccupied and attentive at the same time. Therefore, if we are not seated in the heart, and aligned with our story, the audience will pick up those cues and not trust us. Even if what we have to say will transform their lives, we will have lost them.

In my book *Creating an Abundant Practice*, I talk in great detail about the "sound bite," the "elevator speech," explaining how we can create tailored, neatly wrapped messages in a way that is succinct and informative. However, in a radio or TV interview, we need to have *many* sound bites that articulate not only who we are, but what our business is about and how it differentiates itself from any other business in the same sector. There is only one way to build the interview muscle. It's the same way a musician gets to play at Carnegie Hall—we practice. Here are a few ways we can get into the interview groove:

- Set up mock interview sessions with our family and friends.

- Videotape our sessions. This is an excellent tool that helps us zero in on those little habits that we may not be aware of: how we sit, where we place our hands, or whether we are stiff or slumped down in the chair.

- Take a course in presentation skills, where a professional media coach can pinpoint places that need improvement and help to expedite the learning process.

- Once you feel more comfortable, go on as many interviews as you can, just for the practice.

Radio

Many people are under the impression that being on the radio is easier than being on TV. This is a huge misconception. Why? Perhaps they think since no one will see them they don't have to be concerned with personal appearance. Well, let me tell you, everything matters! We can't hide how we look, even when people can't see us. It shows up in our demeanor. It shows up in our voice.

Don't you think that when we wear our favorite sweater or suit to a radio interview we are going to feel and sound better than if we wear ratty jeans? If our scarf or our belt is too tight, how freely are we going to express ourselves? If our shoes or our bra or our ties are too tight, we may feel contracted. Even if the audience doesn't see us, they will hear us, loud and clear. So it's very important to select the proper attire.

Radio interviewers look for very specific people to have on their show. They do not select their guests randomly; there is a method to their madness.

Claire Papin, an interviewer on Sirius Satellite Radio, says that she looks for people she can easily talk to. She isn't interested in people who will try to challenge her or try to create arguments on the show. She wants to create a harmonic convergence, so to speak. Claire says, "I can tell when the people have taken the time to connect with themselves first—whether they meditate, perform hatha-yoga exercises, or simply take a moment to connect with themselves before the interview.

"It doesn't matter what they do," Claire continues, "it's that they have opened their hearts and minds to the interview process, and as a result, they become delightful, spontaneous guests." [2]

Jessie Dillon, who presents *The Good Life* show, also on Sirius Radio, says he only looks for people who are passionate about what they do and who dwell in "pristine waters." By that he means, "people who are pristine, authentic in their actions." He says, "I'm not interested in people who want to sell or schlep anything, because my audience will be turned off by that kind of information. I'm looking for passionate educators, not salesmen or saleswomen." [3]

A few more things to remember while on the radio:

- Listen to the interviewer and answer only the questions he or she is asking. Don't go off on tangents. The audience picks up on your listening skills immediately.

- Speak into the microphone from the right distance. If you are too far away, the audience will have trouble hearing you. If you're too close, the sound can be jarring and distracting.

- Be articulate. Pronounce your words. Do not slur them or swallow them as you deliver your material.

- Match your energy to the interviewer's. Many times, I've heard a show where the interviewer is exuding a lot of energy and the person being interviewed sounds like he or she is asleep. The only time you do not want to match the interviewer's energy level is when the *interviewer* sounds asleep!

- Check the sound levels on each microphone, so that you and the interviewer both have the same sound quality. If the interviewer has a better microphone, and their voice sounds crisp and articulate while the interviewee's voice sounds weak and muffled, bring it to their attention. Hopefully, they will provide you with a better mike.

- Do not pause too long as you think about a reply to a question. Radio audiences are very different from TV audiences. They have no patience for the "pregnant pause" and may tune to another station if the dialogue isn't flowing.

TV

Obviously, when you are doing a television interview, the visual component is key. Therefore you want to look your best, by wearing clothes that are appropriate. Wear clothes that are not too bright or too busy. Make sure they are comfortable, so you're not tugging or pulling on anything during the interview. Don't wear white! Wear an off-white or colored shirt. Style your hair in a way that is not too extreme. Remember, the first thing people will notice, before you utter a word, is how you look: your body language, the way you are sitting, and how comfortable or uncomfortable you are in front of the camera. We not only want to sound like an expert, we want to look like one. And that is by coming to the show as a "whole package."

Gary DeRodriguez of Life Design International is an expert on supporting speakers in their TV and live presentations. He says,

> TV is a tough medium. You really have to have your message, your sound bite down. So often the TV interviewer will not be familiar with your business and they will ask you questions that are not even relevant to your business. Other times they'll want to create drama on their show and will want to get controversial. So, you'll need to be very solid in your seat. Know your material inside out. Be able to distill your message in an abbreviated format, which needs to be the heart of your message.

Gary goes on to advise, "A spot on TV can make or break a career. Therefore, have your internal work done before you go on your show. Be in alignment with yourself and your message. If you are incongruent with your words, thoughts, and deeds, your message will just be words and people will feel it." [4]

When our marketing materials, our voice, our visuals, and our audio presentations reflect the heart and soul of who we are, the listening audience will either be attracted to what we have to say, or not. We can't be attached to who listens, who becomes interested, or who turns away. That's not our job. Our job is to be ready with our materials and our presentations, and open our hearts and minds to receive those who come to us.

Now that we understand the need for Our Soulful Collateral, we are ready for Building Bridges—those bridges that connect us to the world we wish to impact.

For Further Contemplation

1. What words describe what you do from the highest perspective?

2. Do you have a clear vision of who your audience is?

3. Are you aware of what their concerns are? How do theses concerns relate to your service or what your business offers? Are you familiar with their questions? Are you answering them appropriately?

4. Do your marketing materials resonate with your audience? How do you know?

5. When you speak on the radio or on TV, how do you sound? Do you sound timid? Secure? Cocky? How are you coming across? Is there excitement, passion, and honesty in your delivery?

6. Are you confident about articulating "your story" when you share it?

7. On a scale from 1 to 10, how would you rate your total self-package—your look, your clothes, your hair, your confidence, and your ability to articulate the information you want to get across?

8. Where and how can you make improvements?

CHAPTER 10

BUILDING BRIDGES

Everything in our world is connected to everything else.

— Gregg Braden

Building Bridges is where we move from conceptual thinking to action orientation. It is where we take everything we have learned from the previous chapters, and trust that we have successfully imbibed, synthesized, and integrated these learnings into our consciousness. Once we have achieved this integration, we can begin to construct the bridges that connect us to the larger world—the wonderful world of nodes, clusters, hubs, and influencers; the world of alliances that give us the added boost and value we need, to move forward toward that which we want to attain.

Why build bridges? No man, no woman is an island. Of course, Tom Hanks may be the exception as the Federal Express inspector who finds himself deserted on an island in the movie *Cast Away*. But that is an exception! What business, what individual, has ever succeeded without the support and creative collaboration of at least one other person or one other company?

There are, of course, people who are more adept than others at magnetizing these bridges. We will meet some of them later in this chapter. In the interim, if you are someone who is hesitant when it comes time to "reach out and touch someone," as the saying goes, my hope is that by the end of the chapter you will find this practice easier, less dubious, and perhaps even exhilarating.

The first step in building bridges is to understand network science.

NETWORK SCIENCE

Network science is the knowledge of complex systems and processes that exhibit network behavior. The term *network science* originated from a study done by the National Research Council for the U.S. Army.[1] (I've been unable to identify the year the study was conducted. In view of their findings, it is interesting to note that an idea, even from its inception, can be used for good or for evil.)

The Council discovered that networks are indispensable to the defense of the United States. And that there is no discipline that better offers the fundamental knowledge necessary to design large, complex networks in a predictable manner.

Since the study, countless books on network science have been written, among them *Social Network Analysis: Methods and Applications (Structural Analysis in the Social Sciences)* by Stanley Wasserman, Katherine Faust, and Dawn Iacobucci, and *Linked: The New Science of Networks* by Albert-Laszlo Barabasi.[2]

Network science is the life and breath of our business. It nourishes the seeds of expansion, and opens up avenues that might otherwise seem inconceivable. The application of network science to business outreach stems from a call, a passion, and the need to bridge and form meaningful partnerships with other people, be they friends, acquaintances, or organizations that connect us to our target audience. This holds true whether we are an osteopathic doctor, a contractor, a realtor, the CEO of a Fortune 500 company, or a rock band.

From the spectrum of elements inherent in network science, the ones we will explore in detail are *nodes, hubs, clusters, links,* and *influencers.*

A *node* is a noun: a person, a group of people, an organization, even an animal or a computer. For example, a node could be the shoe salesman at a department store, the animal shelter, or the local bar association.

A *hub* is a large node. Yahoo! and Google are Internet hubs because they connect to millions of nodes, and clusters, and other hubs. The American Bar Association is a hub because it is the umbrella organization for all their American chapters. American Airlines and all the airlines are hubs, because of their size and connectivity.

A *cluster* is a group of three or more nodes or hubs that are associated with each other. One cluster could be six local businesses coming together to raise money for a family in need, or four healing centers working together to present a holistic health fair.

A *link* is the line that connects all the elements of a network. It is the connection that bridges the nodes, clusters, and hubs to form the network. For instance, a link can be the bond between two people, the affiliation between all the chapters of the American Bar Association, or the tie that connects the cluster of businesses raising money for the needy family.

The influencer can be a friend, a family member, or an acquaintance who assists us in linking with the nodes, clusters, and hubs we want to associate with.

Let's walk through a scenario and bring these seeming fragments of tangling particulars together. Imagine a musical group called the Hummingbirds. The Hummingbirds are a node. The reason they are not considered more than a node is that the group is not well known; their fan base is limited. Now, let's say the Hummingbirds link up with another musical group, the Serpents, also an unknown band. The two musical groups, the two nodes, join forces and tour together.

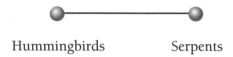

Hummingbirds   Serpents

A third band, the Green Machine, is asked to join the tour. Now you have a cluster: Three or more nodes or hubs connecting to each other. Clearly, by becoming a cluster, they will make a larger impact. The more nodes, the more bands that come together, especially if they are good, solid bands, the wider the outreach, the bigger and better the buzz. Woodstock was a perfect example. When there is more buzz, we increase our visibility, our fan base, and we sell more merchandise, whether CDs, t-shirts, or tickets.

Green Machine

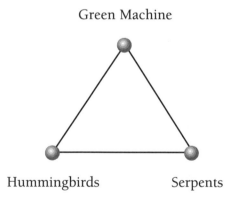

Hummingbirds   Serpents

A hub, in this scenario, would be a record company. Why is a record company a hub? Because it's big! It has the ability to connect lots of nodes, clusters, and hubs: local and regional radio stations (nodes and clusters), television shows, record stores, magazines, and touring companies (hubs). Imagine the growth the Hummingbirds would experience if they linked with two hubs, by signing with a record company *and* a touring agency.

In Albert-Laszlo Barabasi's *Linked: The New Science of Networks*, he states that "the fittest node will inevitably grow to become the biggest hub."[3]

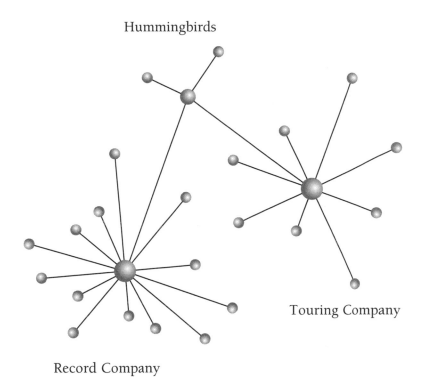

Hummingbirds

Touring Company

Record Company

This is not to say that the only way a musical group can create buzz is through a record company. Look at the recent trend in buying music online rather than in CD format. Thousands of musicians are releasing their music on the Web to be downloaded, and doing quite well aligning with satellite radio and Internet hubs like Sirius and XM Radio and CD Baby—and becoming hubs themselves.

What Is the Fastest Way to Become a Hub?

Give something away, for *free*, that has dynamic value!

Since we're on the topic of music, let's take the Grateful Dead as an example. They are one of the most beloved rock bands ever to have graced the stage and our ears. Think about it! Forty years after they emerged in the sixties, their music still sells, still resonates with listeners around the world.

It's no idle speculation that one of the reasons the Grateful Dead became popular so quickly, besides the fact that they were outstanding musicians, was that they allowed their fans to tape their concerts and trade and copy their tapes. It was their strong belief in their music, trust in their fans, and the fact that they were aware of the bigger picture that powered their success. They knew this sharing of music would increase their exposure and popularity. And their music did spread, like crazy! It didn't take long before the Dead gained international fame, earning millions of dollars, despite their investment in an approach that many people thought might have been a substantial loss.

Giveaways

Think about the stores and banks that give away gifts to lure you into their establishments; the airlines that give you points toward a free ticket; credit-card companies that promise you no interest for a year, the cable companies that offer free service to get you hooked into their programs. Like it or not, these giveaway concepts work!

Last year, during Christmas, the downtown mall in Santa Fe filled their aisles with thirty-some outside merchants. There were artists, craftspeople, card stands, stuffed animals, and pottery booths. I remember walking around the mall to check out the booths, and noticed that one of the booths had a huge crowd around it. As I got closer, I could see several children jumping up and down, very excited. When I was in clear view, I saw that the booth sold inexpensive jewelry and two ladies were giving away free gold bracelets to the children. Those kids were so happy with their little gifts, which in turn made the parents happy, that the news spread throughout the mall. Not to mention the fact that the parents didn't have to reach into their pockets, yet again, to purchase this gift.

Just on the other side of the mall, a similar jewelry stand had only three people standing outside their booth munching on popcorn. No one was waiting in line to buy jewelry and no one was giving anything away.

Find something that has value in your business that you know your audience will appreciate—and give it away. It could be a book, a tele-class, a bottle of your skin-care product, or a free fifteen-minute massage. Don't worry about your initial financial investment. It will come back to you tenfold. Just remember, the offering from your inventory, whatever it is, must have enough substance and integrity to be worth stepping forward and giving away in the first place.

SIX-DEGREE INFLUENCERS

Now, let's say you are a node, a person with a fabulous workshop that you want to introduce to your local hospital and their staff (the hub), because in your heart you know this introduction and ultimate partnering will benefit you both. The only problem is, you don't know anyone within the hub (the hospital) who could introduce you to the person you want to meet.

When this is the case, you need to find an *influencer* to help you. The influencer is the person who may be six degrees or less from knowing the person you want to be introduced to.

"Six degrees of separation" is the idea that anyone on the planet can be connected to any other person on the planet through a chain of acquaintances that has no more than six intermediaries. There was a powerful movie called *Six Degrees of Separation*, starring Will Smith, that illustrates this principle in dramatic form.[4]

While the exact number of links between people differs depending on the population involved, it is generally found to be relatively small. Hence, six degrees of separation is somewhat synonymous with the idea that we actually live in a very small world.

The trivia game "Six Degrees of Kevin Bacon" is based on a variation of the concept of the small-world phenomenon[5] and states that any actor can be linked, through his or her film roles, to Kevin Bacon. The game requires a group of players to try to connect any film actor in history to Kevin Bacon as quickly as possible and in as few links as possible.

Another way to look at this is, you may be only six degrees away from Oprah, but would she let you borrow her iPod? It all depends on the influencers that connect you to her network.

A SIX-DEGREE FLUKE

A past client of mine, Karl (the node in this example), wanted to meet the executive director of the local hospital (the hub), to introduce the director and her staff to his workshop series, "Compassion Fatigue." Karl knew his workshops would be ideal for the hospital staff, but he didn't know anyone at the hospital who could introduce him to the director.

A few weeks passed and Karl was invited to attend a golf tournament. While having lunch with several golfers, Karl was describing his Compassion Fatigue workshops and his desire to offer them to the local hospital. One of the men at the table just happened to be the cousin of the executive director Karl was trying to meet. Karl was blown away. That man became the influencer. Through this link, Karl met the executive director, and has since made several presentations to the hospital staff.

Karl was indeed lucky to have run into the director's cousin. It was clearly a fluke. However, we don't have to depend on flukes. How do we find these influencers when they don't show up magically? We think strategically and do the research.

RESEARCHING THE DEGREES

There are various ways we can research these six degrees. What is most important in this process is to become the "positive deviant" and think outside and beyond the box.

Stephen, a man I met at a film festival, recently finished a movie script he had written for a particular star. He was depressed because he didn't know how to contact this actress, who like all celebrities was surrounded by agents, managers, and PR specialists protecting her privacy. Nevertheless, Stephen was on a mission. I suggested he find out where the actress spends her time outside of the industry, where the cadre of protectors and barbed wire are not as prevalent. "Research the charity groups she may be associated with and cares about," I suggested.

Stephen found out from her Internet fan club that the star was an environmental advocate. He began searching all the environmental charity organizations where she might donate her time or be a spokesperson. It just so happened that Stephen was also interested in environmental issues and was already affiliated with an advocacy group near his home. He found out that she was going to speak at one of the organization's fundraisers. Stephen went, of course, and managed to strike up a conversation with the star. She was intrigued with Stephen's story, and asked him to send a copy of his script to her agent.

The actress read Stephen's script and loved it. It's all still up in the air as to when the film will be made. There is the complication of raising money, finding the right director, the producer. But the good news is, the star is interested. She and her agent are shopping the story and Stephen is now working full-time at the environmental organization where they met. He knows that if the movie is meant to be made—it will be. All he has to do is be patient and persistent. At least he did his due diligence and made the connection.

Using an Influencer or a "Weak Tie" to Find Jobs

Mark Granovetter, an American sociologist best known for his work in social-network theory and in economic sociology, has referred to the influencer as the "weak tie," and discusses this in his book *The Strength of Weak Ties*.[6]

The words *weak tie* may sound confusing as a way to describe someone of influence. But stay with me here. In Granovetter's "Getting a Job: A Study of Contacts and Careers," he shows that our relationship to family members and close friends ("strong ties") will not supply us with as much diversity of knowledge as our relationship to acquaintances, distant friends, and the like (weak ties).

To illustrate Granovetter's idea, let's say you are a computer consultant looking to reach more clients. You wouldn't ask your computer friends (your strong ties) to give you leads. You would seek out people or groups that are not in the same business, who are more diverse and may have the need for your service, like the charity organization you are affiliated with or the basketball team you play with on weekends. Why? Because those hubs have a higher probability of needing a computer consultant. They would become, according to Granovetter, your weak ties and strong allies.

MAGNETIC BUILDERS

One person who has no trouble connecting the dots and establishing those weak ties is former president William Jefferson Clinton. Regardless of one's political affiliation, there is no finer example of a personal magnetism capable of attracting clusters and hubs and creating mega-bridges than Bill Clinton.

I heard Mr. Clinton mention, on *Larry King Live*, about how his entire life had changed after successfully healing from a quadruple coronary artery bypass in 2004. After the operation, he said, the desire to serve people in crisis was now paramount in his mind. As a result, Clinton formed the William Jefferson Clinton Foundation. The foundation is an international nonpartisan initiative to bring the world's best minds and most distinguished problem solvers together. It focuses on global issues such as energy and climate change, health, economic empowerment, ethnic and religious reconciliation, and alleviation of poverty.

Since Clinton launched the organization, he has raised over a billion dollars to support these initiatives. But he didn't do it alone, of course. He brilliantly allied with other concerned leaders: Bill Gates of Microsoft, Fox News' Rupert Murdoch, Prime Minister Tony Blair, Starbucks CEO Jim Donald, TNT CEO Peter Bakker, the king and queen of Jordan, Oprah, former president Bush, and the singer Bono, to name a few.[7]

Besides Clinton's desire to support people in crisis, his other motivating factor was the potential effectiveness for such a coalition. While president, Clinton had certainly been in a position to meet global leaders and connect with developing countries, but that position also had limiting parameters. Congressional bills that he was passionate about had taken months, sometimes years, to pass, if they got passed at all. "Now," he said, "I have total freedom to work with and bridge with anyone I want, at my own pace. When you have people who are committed to changing the world with you, nothing seems impossible!" [8]

The Goodie Stand

Needless to say, we don't need to connect with millionaires to create a powerful bridge. Johnnie, nine years old, had a thriving lemonade business on a busy corner of his subdivision in Livonia, Michigan. His friend Sarah, also nine, had a popcorn stand on another corner, and was just as busy. Even though they were both doing well, and had loyal followings, Sarah thought it might be a cool idea to team up with Johnnie and go into business together. Johnnie thought it would be a cool idea too.

At the time of their merger, another neighbor, Gwen, approached them. Gwen loved making chocolate-chip muffins and wanted to join in on the fun. Johnnie and Sarah thought Gwen's muffins would be an awesome addition to the stand. Gwen was so happy to join them, she came to the stand the next day with three dozen of her delicious muffins, trailed by her parents, eight folding chairs, and a large umbrella to protect customers from the sun while they munched on their goodies.

Word spread quickly around the neighborhood that "The Goodie Stand" had expanded. The neighbors flocked, and within days, the stand's audience tripled. So did the young entrpreneurs' income. Consciously or unconsciously, these children understood the significance of building bridges. And they learned how exciting a business venture can be when everyone contributes something of value.

Networking Groups

Networking groups are a powerful resource for building bridges because they integrate a diverse population. Essentially, any group of people who meet to share an interest, a concern, a hobby, or an activity can potentially function as a networking group. Whether it's your local political association, your church, or your Friday-night bowling league, see the groups you belong to as an opportunity to make new connections.

One of my favorite networking groups in the U.S. is the Katonah Study Group, based in Katonah, New York. They have magnificently connected the alternative-medicine world with the traditional-medicine world. By bringing medical doctors, dentists, gynecologists, and physical therapists together with Holographic Repatterners, Reiki practitioners, and other alternative healers, they bridge the gap between these two sets of approaches. Their forum sets the tone for complementary-medicine practitioners and MDs alike to learn about each other, discover how they can work together, and create a more comprehensive approach through which they can better serve their clients.

INTERNET HUBS

Just look at the sheer volume of visitors that Match.com, MySpace, CD Baby, eBay, Craigslist, and Amazon.com attract to their sites. They are the kings, the royalty of hubs on the Net. Businesses are catching on quickly to this kind of bridging on the Web and offering affiliate partnerships. An affiliate program means that if you promote a business on your website, and that business makes money, you receive a percentage from that referral, and vice versa. Just make sure the business is on the up-and-up and that what they say they are going to do, they follow through on.

There are chat-room hubs, dating-service hubs, bookstore hubs, travel-site hubs. The list goes on and on. Whether it is your desire to meet partners of the same or opposite sex, buy or sell items, purchase shareware, or become an affiliate partner, these Internet portals open doors and opportunities that you could never unlock without the Web. Take advantage of them. That is exactly why they exist.

In a Nutshell

With a few clicks, we can meet people around the block, in the next city or state, or in the most distant country. We can e-mail or pick up the phone and introduce ourselves, break the ice, establish friendships, and create magnificent partnerships. As these doors of opportunity open, we as spiritual marketers need to be conscious not only of our individual potential, but of our global potential. We want to bridge our businesses with people we trust and who trust us. Only then will we establish a network of flow that brings substance, support, resources, energy, and passion from all directions.

The process of building bridges, whether for financial gain or philanthropic purposes, releases us from the narrow confines of our secular lives and opens us to broader perspectives. Once we understand the magic of linking, we see our lives expand, our businesses prosper, and our hearts swell. By committing to this evolutionary agenda, we consciously use our collective wisdom for the highest good.

Opening to this kind of sharing creates the impetus and becomes the catalyst for Leveraging Our Assets, the next step in our initiation process.

FOR FURTHER CONTEMPLATION

1. Are you magnetizing the bridges you want? If not, what is preventing you from establishing these connections?

2. What implications does networking have for how you offer your product or service?

3. What nodes and hubs could you link with that would create "win-win" affiliations?

4. Is there an influencer that could help you connect to those nodes and hubs that you want to associate with?

5. What Internet hubs would be beneficial for you to link with?

6. What could you give away in your business that would be of value to your audience?

7. Are there untapped networking possibilities you could explore in your area? What networking groups could you affiliate with? If there isn't one close to you, could you start one?

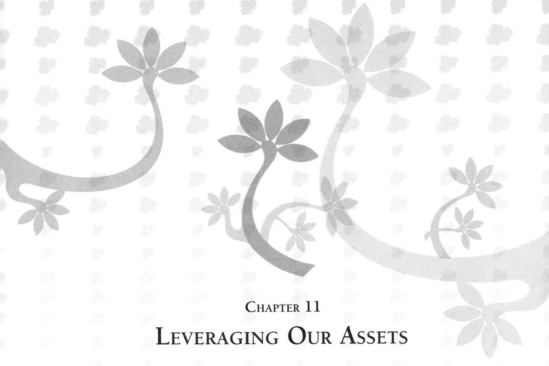

Chapter 11

Leveraging Our Assets

*Of all the things that can have an effect on your future, I believe
personal growth is the greatest. We can talk about sales growth,
profit growth, asset growth, but all of this probably will
not happen without personal growth.*

— Jim Rohn, self-help author

Fine-tuning our businesses, knowing what our business does well and where it needs improvement, is an art and a science in and of itself. There will always be aspects of our profession that need altering—whether it's looking at our day-to-day operations, our employees, our marketing materials, or our technical requirements. At the same time we observe and address these business concerns, we also need to care for our personal growth, so that our own evolution parallels our ever-evolving careers. The attention we give to both these facets, even while they shift from week to week and month to month, gives us the proper footing, the leverage that empowers us to be of significant influence in the marketplace.

How Do We Get There?

We get there by being honest with ourselves. By taking a hard, close look at every single aspect of our business and finding those places that need more structure, more space, more fun, and more balance. For instance, if we are a small-business owner and we know we are good at handling the broad strokes, we need to find someone who enjoys and is proficient at performing the details. If our strength lies in working on the fine points, we need to find someone whose gifts lie in being visionary. If we know that our office will run more efficiently by having a secretary organize our appointments, we hire one.

It's a dance, where, at times, we move forward; at times, we move backward, sometimes taking the lead, sometimes following. Emulating the dynamism of Nataraj in our workplace, we begin to dance with our partners, our employees, and the consultants we employ. Even if we don't perfect all the steps, we are more in sync, more in the flow. By participating in this dance fully we notice right away when we are out of alignment, when it's time to stop or pause to reflect. If we are in doubt as to what the next step should be, we can ask for guidance. We search for the best support to create the leverage necessary.

Leverage, according to the dictionary, means to take a position from which one is able to bring energy and movement to bear on a situation. Applied to the world of business, leverage can mean to improve one's speculative capacity, to take *positional advantage*. Our first impression may be to think positional advantage means taking advantage of other people or the need to be competitive in some way. But this is not the case. Positional advantage means that we take the appropriate steps to create the best scenario. In this way, we have the greatest vantage point and assurance as we move forward.

An *asset* is that which is useful and contributes to the success of something. There are professional assets like property, ownership of goods and services, and then there are personal assets. Personal assets are not just our skills; they include our point of view or inner stance. We leverage these assets by being diligent, and putting forth the right effort.

There are experts who can provide us with ways to cultivate, recognize, and leverage our assets. The question is, what kind of leverage are we looking for? And who are the experts who can show us?

ALTERNATIVE SUPPORT SYSTEMS

There are hundreds of qualified business consultants who can support our next steps. There are financial, technical, and managerial advisors. There are courses where we can learn about uncontested market spaces, the price corridor of the mass, analytical tools and frameworks. And while these topics are relevant in our business, in this chapter on leveraging we will *not* be covering those particular points.

Instead, I would like to explore three nontraditional, alternative approaches: systems that leverage our assets from a psychological, emotional, and spiritual perspective. The three I would like to introduce are *astrology*, *astrocartography*, and *feng shui*. Why these three systems? Because they have, over the years, provided me with the necessary edge that keeps me alert, and on top of my game. We need this edge to manifest equanimity in our daily affairs, and to deal with the challenges that pop up when least expected.

These resources have given me insight into the complex world we live in, insight into my own flaws and gifts. They have supported me as I've made both small and dramatic adjustments that at first were difficult, but in the end provided me with great solace. They have also helped me to see my clients in the highest light, so that I can serve them from a place of appreciation and respect.

ASTROLOGY

Astrology is an ancient system that correlates the flow of life on earth with the ever-changing patterns of the planets. It is a psychological tool that can be used with great subtlety in describing personality, the shifting cycles of our lives, and the opportune opening of pathways through which we can fulfill our calling, our destiny.

Depending on our natal chart, which pictures when, where, and what time we were born, we will inherently have certain characteristics, certain qualities, and—whether we like it or not—specific challenges. The planetary configuration that we are born with is like our DNA. And like DNA, it is not deterministic; it is shaped by and through time and events. It shows us, via the interweaving of transits and progressions, the outer events, themes, and trends that relate to our individual lives—and to no one else's.

As the West's oldest and most detailed language for describing the qualities and movements of energy, astrology can teach us many things about ourselves, our family, those we work with, and the principles of timing and positioning.

I have used astrology to support my clients in numerous ways. For instance, one woman I was coaching had a Scorpio sun. Her tendency, as with many Scorpios, was to communicate in a way that was at times abrupt, cryptic, and stinging, like the scorpion's notorious tail. People with this Scorpio aspect don't mean to speak in a hurtful way; it is simply how this aspect can express itself. Unaware of this trait and how it affects other people, my client was baffled when she received negative feedback from a presentation she had prepared. Participants had commented that she appeared cold and angry. With this astrological characteristic brought to her attention, she could make the appropriate adjustments and soften her approach.

Another client was having difficulty staying on course. She couldn't focus on the projects she wanted to complete. When I found out that she had a Pisces sun and a Pisces moon, it helped me understand her challenge. Pisces, a water sign, is mutable and deeply emotional, even to the point of self-sacrifice. Having both sun and moon in Pisces doubled the impact of these traits. To keep herself from drowning or drifting in the waves of life, she clearly needed more structure, more containers to support her. Once we created the life jacket she needed, with tools like more discipline in her schedule and a date book for her appointments, her business took off and she was well on her way, swimming with the current.

The Four Alignments

Jade Luna, a gifted astrologer from Southern California, says that there are four alignments that are particularly useful to know about when dealing with our careers: Mercury retrogrades, Mars conjunctions and oppositions, waxing Moon, and Venus–Jupiter conjunctions and trines.[1]

Here's a description of how they work.

Mercury Retrograde

Mercury retrograde is an alignment that takes place about four times a year. Of all the planetary configurations, this one creates the most problems in the work world. During Mercury retrograde, the planet Mercury appears first to stand still, then to move backward. This Mercury "slowdown" becomes problematic on many levels. Mercury rules over communication and mechanical devices: computers, cars, and telephones. The slowdown also affects the clarity of our everyday attention, our practical decision making, and our ability to communicate and express ourselves.

I am particularly watchful when Mercury goes retrograde since my sun sign is in Gemini, which is ruled by Mercury. During this transit, I am especially cautious of the words I use. I check and double-check e-mails, letters, checks that I write, and any form of communication. I do not sign contracts, because the day a contract is signed is its actual "birthday" and sets the pattern for the future of that agreement. I do not plan big moves, and I drive very carefully, as accidents are more likely to happen during this time.

Mars Conjunctions, Squares, and Oppositions

Mars is the planet of war and of anger, of impulsiveness and thoughtless self-assertion, and has the potential to create massive problems for short periods. Conjunctions, squares and oppositions are aspects of great force. When there is a conjunction involving Mars, it is usually a time of difficult or opposing forces that are coming to the surface. When Mars is in a challenging aspect with the Sun, it creates conflicts regarding leadership and authority. Therefore, if we haven't dealt with these subconscious issues of the ego, we will draw to ourselves those people who embody these issues for us—so we can work through them. If we keep magnetizing those people who bring up the very scenarios of struggle that infuriate us, it's because we haven't dealt with them ourselves.

The most difficult time of the year for people in business is when Mars squares, opposes, or conjoins Saturn, which brings the cool strength of Saturnine containment, structure, and limitation into direct confrontation with Mars' impetuosity. These are times of heavy stress, delays, and arguments that can permanently derail partnerships. Knowledge about Mars is enormously important for maintaining a happy environment.

The Waxing Moon

From the tiny sliver of the new Moon, the waxing Moon grows bigger and brighter, night by night, until it culminates in the full Moon. The waxing Moon is a force that pulls in an upward motion toward growth and expansion. The energy of the Moon has to do with emotion, nurturance, and a sense of being "at home." The waxing Moon is great for signing contracts and hiring new people; the Moon's increasing energy creates a feeling of comfort and may be one of the greatest alignments to pay attention to for keeping clients in a joyful atmosphere.

JUPITER AND VENUS TRINES AND CONJUNCTIONS

Trines are angles of 120 degrees that connect two planets in signs of the same element. Trines are traditionally considered harmonious, easeful, balanced, and auspicious; conjunctions, for their part, bring energies into strong interaction. Jupiter and Venus are often called "the great beneficents" among the planets, as their harmonious aspects are the greatest alignments for all kinds of success, financial and otherwise. When these alignments occur, it is said that Jupiter takes the form of the remover of obstacles, and Venus takes the form of the bestower of prosperity. These are the greatest alignments for starting a new business. Signing contracts during one of these Jupiter–Venus aspects creates an incredible foundation for financial success—in fact, for flourishing in every form. As the waxing Moon creates a happy atmosphere, Jupiter–Venus trines and conjunctions assure abundance.

ASTROCARTOGRAPHY

Astrocartography is an extension of astrology. It is a system also based on a person's natal astrological chart, but with a very specific focus: it offers a way to determine geographically where an individual's inherent potential can be most fully realized. It is an indicator as to where a person is best suited to live, work, and find love, creative or intellectual fulfillment, good health, and financial vitality.

With the efficiency of computers and the Internet, our lives have sped up, our communications are faster, and we are more mobile. No longer are we at the same job or living in the same house for thirty years, like our parents. Our generation moves through a succession of career changes, untethered to a designated location—which in some ways makes our lives a blessing, and in other ways, a curse.

Since we are not tied down to one location, we are free to live anywhere we choose. However, if where we live does not resonate with our astrological influences, no matter how great our business is, we will not have the leverage necessary to manifest our highest aspirations. So when we settle down to start a career, aligning energetically with the geographical area will support our success.

Given the birth chart and the current planetary configurations, the question of where to live to experience greater expansion and awareness can be answered by a qualified astrocartographer.

Gilbert Pichinich, a gifted San Francisco astrologer and astrocartographer, shares two stories about clients who came to him wanting to find new homes. Names and some details have been changed to protect the privacy of his clients.[2]

A Move to the Southwest

Joanna, 52 years old, lived in Orange County, New York. She was bored, lifeless. She knew she needed to move, but had no idea where. She was also longing to find a partner.

After looking at her chart, Gilbert saw that Saturn was on the cusp of her seventh house, a placement that can be an obstruction to a relationship. He suggested she move to southwestern Arizona, where the ruler of her fifth house (romance and the joy of life) was more prominent in her chart. Jupiter, the planet that expands, was now placed in her fourth house, which represents home (on an outer level) and deep feeling (on an inner level). The aspects in the new location would remove the limitations she was experiencing in New York.

After a series of visits to Scottsdale, Arizona, she decided to move there. And within a few weeks she found a job that she loved and a partner she is still with.

When Gilbert spoke to Joanna recently, her energy was entirely different from when she lived in New York. She told him she had never been happier in her life, and that she never would have moved to Arizona had it not been for her astrocartography reading.

MOVING WEST

John, a man in his mid-fifties, had lived in Baltimore for several years. John was a great healer, a master Reiki practitioner and a shaman, who at the time could hardly pay his rent. Because he had Venus and Mercury in the ninth house, he had great teaching potential. However, the location where he was living, in Baltimore, did not have the right aspects, nor was it conducive to the recognition of his gifts.

Gilbert suggested John move to Southern California where he'd experience the increased influence of Uranus, which represents intellectual creativity, and the influence of the Sun on his ascendant in Leo, the ruler of creative expression. John made the move. And since his sun sign was also in Leo, instead of the five-watt life he was living in Baltimore, his life was now supercharged with 200-watt energy. Now in alignment with the planets that supported his gifts of healing and teaching, John took off like a rocket. And he started making more money than he'd ever made in his life—doing what he does best.

WHEREVER YOU GO, THERE YOU ARE

Moving, of course, is not a cure-all. Changing our location does not change our mind, our basic approach to life, or the gifts we came in with. The "geographical cure" is not something we undertake as an escape from ourselves. After all, as the saying goes, "wherever you go, there you are."

Knowing this, we take a careful look at our urge for going. Whether we go or stay, we need to know the reasons. If, after examining your motives and your alternatives, you find you need to stay in an area where your aspects are not the best, there may be karmic reasons why you cannot leave. Perhaps you owe someone your time, your love and support; maybe the time is not right. Maybe there are factors that are not yet visible, still in development in the womb of time and space, that have to manifest before outer movement is possible. Or maybe . . .

We never know. And then again, sometimes we do.

On the other hand, there are ways to deal with these conditions, ways to live and dance harmoniously with the forces of the place in which we find ourselves. One of these ways is to incorporate the principles of feng shui into our lives.

FENG SHUI

Although cynics abound, claiming that feng shui is a superstition and nothing more, there are plenty of realtors, architects, builders, and interior designers using the principles of feng shui. The *Los Angeles Times* reports that News Corp., Coca-Cola, Proctor & Gamble, Hewlett-Packard, and Ford Motors are following suit. And rumor has it that "The Donald," Donald Trump, uses feng shui in many of his hotels and casinos.

I have personally walked into rooms and known immediately that feng shui had been used to color the walls or to place furniture in certain configurations. There is a distinct feeling of energy moving freely around the space. There is a sense of clarity, and sparseness without feeling cold. When a friend came to my house and made some minor changes using feng-shui principles, stagnant rooms became places of noticeable vibrancy and my business doubled. So, regardless of what the cynics say, I believe!

Feng shui (pronounced "fung shway") is an ancient Chinese practice of placement and arrangement to achieve harmony in our everyday environments, and to align our possessions, our homes, land, and landscaping with the creative life energy, known as *chi* or *qi*.

The written Chinese character *feng* means "wind," and *shui* means "water." These two characters together, *feng shui* ("wind and water"), describe the flow and accumulation of chi. Feng shui is the art and the science of cultivating positive chi energy in our daily lives, and is a synthesis of geographical, philosophical, mathematical, aesthetic, and astrological ideas.

The *ba gua* (or *pa kua*), an octagonal diagram, is one of the main tools used in feng-shui analysis. Each direction on the octagon (north, northeast, east, and on around the directional "clock") is associated with a specific color, a particular part of the body, and other elements. In the construction of a home or the laying out of a functional space, the qualities associated with each direction determine the most appropriate placements for rooms and activities—where the "wealth" corner, the "relationship" corner, the "community and family" corner are located in a structure. The birth date of the person who will occupy a home or business space is also considered in making decisions.

By mapping the ba gua onto a home, office, or construction site, information about correct orientation and placement can be gleaned. Objects such as mirrors, crystals, wind chimes, fountains of flowing water, hanging plants, and folding screens can be used to redirect, reflect, or shift energy in a space.

Eiko Okura, an interior designer and feng-shui practitioner of the Black Hat lineage, says, "On a mundane level, the process of feng shui helps us to identify and refine our goals. On a transcendental level, the workings of feng shui are magical and mysterious, beyond logic. It teaches us to surrender to the flow of organic and spontaneous creative energy, and forces our mind to expand rather than limit itself and contract." [3] Eiko describes an experience with one of her corporate clients:

> One of my clients started a business with his wife in their basement five years ago and employed the principles of feng shui. Every aspect of the building was feng shui'd: the placement of the building itself, the landscape, the furniture, the color of the furniture, and the color of each wall. I made sure that the CEO's office was in the commanding position, which in some offices is in the center and other times in the wealth corner. Each department, including the reception desk, had to be aligned for the chi to function properly.
>
> Within three years, the company moved from its small rented space to purchasing its own building, and now has a staff of over 200. I am working with the owner and the design team to build their new building and to accommodate more functions and employees. My clients are so convinced that feng shui helped them increase their revenue, they call me before they paint a bathroom or move a chair. It is always exciting, and an honor, to witness feng shui in action and bring success into my clients' businesses. [4]

Controversy Will Always Exist

There will always be controversy! Controversy stimulates us to get clear about our passions, our beliefs. There is controversy regarding politics, religion, the environment, war, marriage, nonmarriage, you name it. There is controversy regarding astrology, astrocartography, and feng shui, as well as other forms of alternative support like massage, acupuncture, reflexology, and life coaching.

Regardless of which ones we choose, we can use these systems as an adjunct to our personal lives and to our businesses. They can be an angle from which we can explore, confirm, or clarify what we are needing at any given moment. They can be a catalyst for change and a way we can learn about others and ourselves. Adding these approaches to our bag of tools gives us the positional advantage we need to stay on the cutting edge, and in the niche we've chosen. Particularly at those times when we need a moment of pause or a second opinion.

Leveraging Our Assets is yet another apex in the journey we've embarked upon. It's the springboard that propels us to embrace the richness of our lives, and to share that wealth with others.

For Further Contemplation

1. What are some of the assets you consider most significant in your-self as a person, or in your business?

2. What are some of the leverage points you use to access your assets or bring them to bear in business situations? Are they serving you? Do you need to find new ones? Do you have a sense of what these new forms of leverage might be?

3. Have you ever used astrology to support you in the past? Are you ambivalent to explore astrology? If so, why?

4. Are you happy where you live? Is the location serving you, and your business?

5. Where have you always dreamed of living? What is stopping you from moving there now, or in the near future? Would it help if you spoke to an astrocartographer?

6. Is the place where you work pleasant? Beautiful? Stimulating? Are the colors in the office vibrant? Boring? Does it invite you to be creative? Friendly? Do you feel contracted in the space? Does the space feed you creatively?

7. What changes could be made in the space that would support you in performing your best?

CHAPTER 12

RESPONDING FROM ABUNDANCE:
SHARING THE WEALTH

Service is the rent that you pay for room on this earth.

— Shirley Chisholm

When I was in rural India in the early seventies, I remember being a passenger in a bicycle rikshaw. My body bopping up and down from the bumpy unpaved roads, my eyes wide open as we passed people of all ages working in the hot fields. Homes made of mud and straw with doorways barely high enough to accommodate the wooden bowls atop the heads of the small women. Couples walking miles just to get water, kids running naked because they had no clothes. And yet, as I passed scene after scene, there was an aura of richness within these people that emanated outward—noticeably. The children were ecstatic playing and working in the fields. Men with no teeth grinned, offering us mangoes and papayas as we rode by. There was such beauty between the particles of dust that blew in our faces.

Arriving back in the States, the first thing I saw when I got off the plane was two kids yelling at the top of their lungs, fighting over a Game Boy. A husband and wife arguing over who was going to eat the last bite of the cheeseburger. *My God,* I thought, *if they only knew how lucky they are.*

And that's when it hit me:

Abundance is an inside job. It has little to do with money or resources. Abundance has to do with our own worth, our spiritual wealth, and the deepest joy. When we know what our true value is, we feel full, bounteous. We can't help but share what we have because our cup is overflowing. Stinginess and selfishness do not enter our consciousness. How could they? Having the recognition of our inner beauty, we respond to the world with generosity and thoughtfulness. We are all too willing to distribute whatever resources we have without hesitation.

You may ask yourself, what is it that I *can* share? For some of us it may well be money, real estate, art, or other tangible investments. For others, it may be a service of some kind, inspiration, intellectual knowledge, or a simple act of kindness or empathic listening. Our society places so much emphasis on material wealth that we undervalue spiritual competency and basic humanity. Why do so many of us wait until there's a catastrophe, a death, or a divorce before we remember what is truly important? So before we ask ourselves the question, *What do I have to offer?* we may need to ask the question, *Why am I here?* When you think about it, we are all living on this planet at this same time, together, for a reason. It is neither an accident nor a coincidence. The people we associate with, live with, work with, run into at the supermarket: they are all in our life for a reason. So, ask yourself, why *are* you here? Is it to simply exist, to feed off of others, off the land? Is it to hoard, to own or to possess? Or is it to share, to bring joy, support, and happiness to yourself and others?

As long as we inhabit this terrain, we can display generosity, or greed. We can go about our business not caring about the people close to us, our employees, our neighbors, or other nations. We can weaken the human spirit by being selfish, acting out one-upmanship—or we can share with each other, equitably and responsibly. The people who understand this principle seem to orbit around Spaceship Earth quite differently from those who do not.

Raphael Kellman, author of *Matrix Healing: Discover Your Greatest Potential Through the Power of Kabbalah*, reminds us why it is imperative that we share our wealth. He says, "When we become proactive in our giving, we overcome our reactive natures if only for an instant. At that moment, the creative force of the universe enters the deepest recesses of our cells and begins the healing process at the most fundamental level." [1] Sharing always enlarges us.

THE UNIVERSAL FLOW

There is a flow that occurs when we make an offering, be it a donation of money, an offering of our work, or a sharing of our God-given talent. The very act of *offering* strengthens the heart, activates a surge of energy within, and propels us to do more, be more, serve more. This act annihilates apathy and imbues us with a sense of purpose.

Making offerings in conjunction with the financial gifts we receive separates the serious business owners from the ones who act "as if." Enlightened entrepreneurs know that when they give a portion of their wealth away, they never have lulls in their business. They understand the universal principle of giving and receiving and acknowledge that when the flow stops, there is something inside *themselves* that stops. And when that happens, it's time to go inside, quiet the mind through meditation or whatever form of self-inquiry one practices, and ask oneself: *What's off? What's not in balance?* The imbalance may be that we have spent too much time or become stuck in one of the three faces of the creative process. Or the imbalance may stem from ignorance, fear, clutching, or just plain self-indulgence.

Encouragingly, I believe there are more conscious business owners today than ever before: entrepreneurs who are not just aware of their immediate surroundings, their partners and their employees, but who give to their community and to organizations that have fewer resources. Some businesses offer a percentage of their weekly or monthly income toward a community service or charity, and ask that their employees participate as well. Their contributions may help fund a local women's shelter or the building of a new teen center. Other employers and employees donate their time on weekends or a few days a month during business hours to support organizations like Habitat for Humanity or environmental concerns, to create community gardens, to educate the public about energy efficiency, water conservation, or health care. There are millions of for-profit and not-for-profit businesses making a difference with contributions like these.

Leadership, initiative, and generosity can occur at all levels of management and income. We can be that CEO, that business owner who subscribes to a philosophy of sharing, with the potential to inspire others around us to find *their* most meaningful form of contribution. When our businesses are blended with a personal commitment to serve the greater good, individual waves of caring can create a tsunami of positive impact.

I would like to describe three business owners who have struggled with this principle, and two businesses that not only understand it, but have provided enormous growth opportunities for their employees and for other businesses and touched thousands of people around the world. These stories are true; the names have been changed to protect the innocent as well as the accountable.

THE DESIGNER

In the early eighties, during the heyday of the dot-com boom, I worked as a consultant for a high-end design firm specializing in animation for the Web. Greg, the owner, was extremely talented, but he didn't understand the principle of "the offering" or the positive response it could evoke with the industry that supported him.

Allow me to elaborate:

Greg was invited to design a logo for an annual fundraiser that would have brought him tremendous exposure as well as name-brand recognition. The not-for-profit organization that wanted him to design a logo was the "mother ship" for all the dot-com companies in Silicon Alley. It was their once-a-year, pull-all-the-stops-out gala. His logo would have been seen by hundreds of people on twenty TV screens throughout the six-room facility where the function was being held, and on the brochure promoting the event.

I explained to Greg that this was the opportunity of a lifetime. It was a chance to give back to the industry that supported him. And while there would be no payment for his design, the volume of publicity and sheer goodwill he would receive would more than compensate for the fact that he was not getting paid. He would never be able to purchase this kind of advertising.

He turned down their request, and said, quite emphatically, "I am not going to waste my time on something I'm not getting paid to do." I begged him to reconsider. When he wouldn't budge, I knew it was only a matter of time before I'd have to stop working with him. I could not in good faith represent someone who didn't understand the principle of the offering, and the opportunity that this particular gift would have brought.

The Ski Resort

There was a wonderful ski resort in the Catskills, where my son and I lived for a year. The resort was a scaled-down replica of a famous ski town in Switzerland. Condominiums and A-frame houses circled the ski hills, and a large community center was the gathering place for kids and parents to drink hot chocolate, order chicken fingers and fries—light cuisine for the cold, hungry athletes. A big brick fireplace warmed skiers coming in from the cold and provided comfort for parents waiting for their kids to return from the slopes. It was heaven on earth. Especially for a single parent who had to work full time!

In the summer, the children would go swimming, throw Frisbees, and trek the hills on their bikes, while the adults luxuriated at the pool. During our first few months in residence there, I would pinch myself: Was this a dream? Was I really living in this oasis?

And then, everything changed.

The owners, realizing they needed to bring in added revenue, decided to market outside the immediate area. They ended up bringing in busloads of college kids on the one hand and middle-class families from the city on the other. Their marketing strategy turned into a disaster. The college kids were rude and obnoxious, bursting drunkenly through the dining hall, taking over the slopes and generating endless accidents.

The owners, who thought their friends from the city would enjoy their weekend getaway, were not pleased. Their well-to-do urban friends were appalled, and eventually stopped coming. The college kids eventually got bored and went to another ski area to wreak havoc. Slowly but surely the inevitable happened and the resort went bankrupt. It was so disappointing to watch this incredible winter wonderland, this beautiful summer retreat, dissolve in front of my very eyes. I spoke to management and tried to reach the owners, but they were not interested in my marketing suggestions.

What could the owners have done differently? To begin with, they could have embraced the local community. They could have had a singles night for skiing, a couples night, a teen night, a family weekend, Halloween parties, Christmas parties, Hanukkah parties (this was the Catskills, after all). Promoting and marketing these ongoing events would have attracted new people, who in turn would have brought their relatives and friends. Another successful strategy would have been to reach out to the nonprofit community. By supporting the charitable organizations through hosting fundraisers—fashion shows, talent shows, ski races, snowboarding competitions—the owners would have received tremendous support on a local level.

When we take this grassroots approach, we truly honor our local community and create a groundswell. Through this inclusive approach, we generate a climate of goodwill and expansion. At the same time, we are fine-tuning an outreach strategy that can be replicated in other communities, other cities, other states and countries—and often becomes an unfailing blueprint for success.

THE TEA SHOP

The Tea Shop, based in downtown Santa Fe, was a "happening hangout" in the center of town. Its fun, relaxed atmosphere was redolent with the fragrance of hundreds of exotic teas; it served delicious vegetarian meals, and was a venue for drum circles, talks and workshops, poetry readings, and holistic practitioners demonstrating their modalities.

The best thing about the Tea Shop was that it stayed open till one in the morning. This was a protocol foreign to most restaurants in Santa Fe. It was a wonderful place to go for late-night brainstorming, the munchies, or simple conviviality.

The owner, Peter, had an open-door policy for local fundraising activities that supported the animal shelter, the hospice, the rape-crisis center, the teen center, and other worthy not-for-profit enterprises. He invited artists to display their paintings on the Tea Shop walls and, unlike the high-priced galleries that took considerable percentages, he refused to take a dime if a picture sold.

And then, one day, I walked into the Tea Shop and everything was different.

The place appeared the same on the surface, but it was as if I was looking at a beautiful corpse whose soul had left its body. The energy in the Tea Shop had shifted. When I asked the young man behind the counter if Peter was in, he told me that Peter had sold the establishment to a man named Bill. I was stunned. But at least this explained the startling change of ambience.

For the next few months, I kept popping into the Tea Shop to see what the new owner was up to, to see if he was making changes, bringing in new teas, transforming the place into something unique, or at least maintaining the quality of service Peter had provided in the past. But the only changes were more dust accumulating on the teapots; no more poetry readings, no exciting art on the walls. There were only dark, gothic paintings on display, with exorbitant price tags. It wasn't long before the business began to drop off and lose money.

It was indeed a sad scenario. Particularly because there were no quiet restaurants in Santa Fe where you could go and sit and have a conversation after ten o'clock at night. Watching the downfall of this establishment underlined a core principle: where there is no heart, no love for the work, when you stop making offerings to the community you reside in, it reflects in your earnings.

Well, enough gloom and doom! Now for something a little more heartwarming. Let's turn to a few examples of business owners who understand responding from abundance, and the fruits of maintaining the right relationship with what they receive.

A New York Law Firm

I heard about this law firm from my friend Frieda. She works as a legal assistant in the firm. Frieda loves her job. She loves the three attorneys she assists, and the other assistants. Frieda gets up early, takes the train from Westchester to the city, comes home late, and never complains about her workload or her coworkers.

Now, I'd like to preface this story by saying that Frieda has extensive experience as a legal assistant and could work for any law establishment in the country. But she loves working for this one. Why? She gets holiday bonuses, time off for vacation; and whenever she is ill and needs a few days to recover, the company insists she take time off, with pay. But it's more than that.

Not only is the firm generous with their long-term dedicated employees; they have a policy that every attorney there must offer a portion of his or her workload pro bono to a not-for-profit—whether sitting on the board or offering legal advice or service to a charity at no charge.

When they have lunch meetings, the extra food get donated to local charities, those who feed the city's unemployed. Every Christmas the entire firm takes turns volunteering to cook at local homeless shelters. And if any attorney from the company passes away, they close their doors, so everyone can attend the funeral.

Now, is it any wonder that this law firm is one of the most successful in New York City?

The White Dog Café

The White Dog Café[2] opened in 1983 in a Victorian brownstone in downtown Philadelphia. As the café's founder, Judy Wicks saw her mission clearly: to blend good food with her concern for the environment, politics, and social issues. Judy's little café on Samson Street has since turned into an international meeting place, known both for its delicious cuisine and for programs and initiatives that have been recognized worldwide.

Here are just a few of the programs Judy has established:

Table Talks is a forum through which speakers can address issues of public concern, and where patrons can sit around a table filled with delicious food and discuss topics such as health-care reform, violence, the environment, foreign policy, cultural diversity, the needs of children and youth, and education.

The Philadelphia Sister Restaurant Project is an initiative that develops "sister" relationships with minority-owned restaurants around the world. This program increases understanding, builds community, and supports minority businesses and cultural institutions. The Sister Project also sponsors tours throughout the world to promote understanding of the restrictions existing restaurants may face in other countries and how U.S. foreign policy affects them.

Urban Retrievers promotes education by mentoring high-school students, teaching tolerance and interconnectedness through storytelling. This program gives voice to the underrepresented, and gives inner-city community tours of local business and artistic entities.

Community Service Days are held throughout the year, volunteering White Dog customers and staff to participate in projects like rehabilitating houses or building community gardens.

Take a Senior to Lunch offers White Dog customers the opportunity to bring a senior to lunch or be matched with a senior who would like to get out more often. Both senior and donor receive half off their total bill.

And if that isn't enough, next door to the White Dog Café is the Black Cat, another establishment created to foster economic justice. The Black Cat sells products made by disadvantaged workers and is a magnificent complement to the White Dog Café, where patrons can see the tangible products of Judy's global efforts.

What Others Say

Victor Heredia, founder and CEO of eLearning Institute, an online organization committed to expanding awareness and education worldwide, principally in Latin America, says:

> There is no greater reward than sharing what you have with others. It goes beyond giving money. It is about taking action and getting involved. Those people who have had access to better education, lifestyles and opportunities in their lives have a responsibility to share their knowledge. This understanding creates better conditions for the planet, distributes our resources, and helps us to remember that we are all in the same boat. This boat is our world. [3]

International speaker and healer Kay Snow Davis served as crisis coordinator and trauma specialist for the disaster-recovery program on the island of Kauai post-Hurricane Iniki. Kay says, "Innately people have a desire to 'do good deeds' but many times have no direction for that intention. If one were to look, they wouldn't have to look far. Many times, the need is right in their backyard." [4]

In addition to being a life coach, Spryte Loriano founded Feed 333, a not-for-profit entity with a global vision committed to nourishing children in three different ways: food for their bodies, education for their minds, empowerment for their spirits. Spryte says: "There is a missing link in service, and that is that most of our role models are great givers but they are not great receivers—in their own lives. When we approach service from a place of knowing, not just believing, our own deservedness to be served, we complete the universal cycle of giving and receiving." [5]

We Don't Have to Wait!

Making offerings, developing social responsiveness, does not have to be an undertaking we make once a year during Christmas or Thanksgiving. Nor do we have to wait until there is a disaster before offering our support to our neighbors—in our own communities, and around the world. There are so many people who need our support right now, in so many ways. Help someone in need, embrace a child whose feelings are hurt, smile at a stranger. Give someone a bouquet or a live plant or a hug when you know they need your attention. Offer a percentage of your wages to a spiritual or environmental cause, a local or global organization. Offer or enhance a service within your community.

When we start responding to the greater world and move out of our insular caves, we automatically create a ripple effect in our own lives, for our families, for our children and our children's children.

Is there a guarantee that this practice will grant monetary success or a more meaningful life? If we are open to it, and respond from this place of inner abundance, we will find ourselves living a richer and fuller existence. Through our offerings we build a more meaningful life—and the entire planet opens up to us and offers us, in return, its bounty, its magnificence, and its perfection.

FOR FURTHER CONTEMPLATION

1. How do you think of abundance? In what ways do you experience richness in your life?

2. What are the gifts or special forms of abundance that you have to share as an individual?

3. What are the gifts or special forms of abundance that your business has to share?

4. Does your business abide by the universal principle of giving and receiving?

5. What are the ways your business gives back to the community? What are some of the ways you could reach out to become more responsive?

6. Do you, or your company, wait until there is a crisis before giving, or do you give on a regular basis?

7. Looking at the ways your business makes offerings to the local or global community, are your offerings effective? Could they be more effective? If so, how?

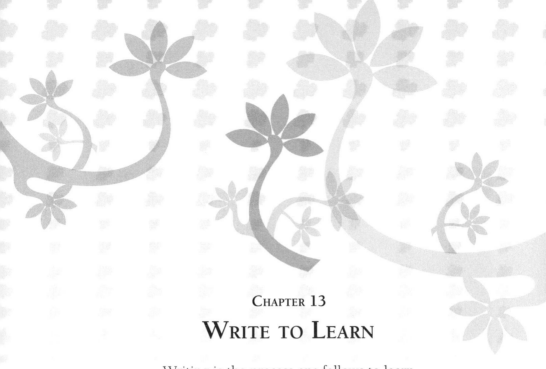

CHAPTER 13

WRITE TO LEARN

Writing is the process one follows to learn
what is already known deep within: it sharpens the spirit,
disciplines the mind and leads to solutions.
In the spaces between words and solitude
observe what happens when words and silence meet.
Words matter. Pay attention.
Write to learn what you know.

— Maryanne Radmacher

This quote is beautifully framed and placed on a wall close to my computer. It reminds me that the only reason I write is to learn what is already inside me, and to discover that which I still have to learn. It is an aide-memoire, a reminder that the only way we can access true information is by listening to the spaces between the words. It is in that space of solitude that the words spring forth.

The process of writing and the reasons we write vary from person to person. Some of us write to explore our artistic potential, to connect with the deepest part of ourselves, to challenge ourselves, to teach, to dare, to fantasize. Others of us write to express our creativity, to engage the heart in ways we cannot reach by plunging into any other activity.

Writing, like other art forms, is a spiritual path; it is a journey that grabs hold of our senses, and takes us for a wild and wondrous ride. If we can trust ourselves to hold on, let go, surf the depths and ride the waves, writing becomes a huge leap into the infinite, taking us to a place where we experience our own divine music—the inner movement that transforms us from solo players to conductors of our own orchestra. It can be a glorious trip out into the abyss, where there are no guideposts, only the matrix of convergence; where the mind, the heart, the fingers, and the body merge, synchronizing into the pulsation of one's own rhythm.

FINDING OUR RHYTHM

Discovering the rhythm and style of your writing takes patience and practice. It's a muscle and an awareness you build and perfect over time. In the same way that you don't go the gym and pick up a two-hundred-pound bar on your first visit, you don't try to write a 450-page book in a week. You nurture and develop your writing capacity; you read other people's work and see what it is in their style that resonates for you. Take notice of what you like, and don't like. When you listen to the voice in the writing that tells you where they're coming from, you hear what rings true. And then, you can go to your writing pad or your computer and allow *your truth* to come through.

Building the writing muscle doesn't have to be painful. Joy can come from this exercise. Especially when you become aware that the fruit of your effort is experienced in the effort itself. You don't just "do" the practice to get the result. You allow the practice of writing and the fruit to become one.

You can start by writing a little bit each day and listening to the way your voice wants to be expressed from the heart, organically, authentically. And then keep writing until your voice surfaces, and you begin to hear it, feel it. When it does show its face, let go, let it rip, and allow those thoughts to cascade out onto the page.

Witnessing your emotions while you write plays a huge part in the progression, because whatever you're feeling will show up on the page. Just try writing a warm, fuzzy letter while you're angry. Or see what happens if you try to write a brochure when, just the day before, someone you love has passed away. Check inside: there may be some other writing to do first, to clear away the emotional cobwebs or tangles.

JOURNALING

Journaling is a wonderful way to get in touch with your own genuine perceptions and your writing rhythms. Just sitting down every day, picking up a pen, and writing down your dreams, or whatever is going through your mind, is one way to allow your innate rhythms to birth themselves.

Julia Cameron uses journaling as a practical way to get in touch with authentic feelings and creative aspirations. In her book *The Artist's Way: A Spiritual Path to Higher Creativity*, she suggests writing what she calls *morning pages*. Simply put, morning pages are three or more pages of writing in longhand, using stream of consciousness. All we have to do is sit down and allow whatever thoughts happen to be swimming around in our psyche to move through our fingers and land on the page.

These pages are not meant to be brilliant, although sometimes they might be. They are meant to open up blocked energy and patterns that we hold on to dearly, so our words and our thoughts flow without obstruction.[1]

When Is the Best Time to Write?

The best time to write is when you have the fewest distractions. When there are no phone calls or outside noises to pull you away. It may be after a deep meditation when your intuition is at its peak and your senses are heightened. It may be in the early morning, or late at night when everyone is asleep.

There are some people who hunker down and are very happy writing in one place day after day. They find comfort in knowing they have their own space, in seclusion from the outside world. Other people need to move around. I know a writer who changes locations every week. He says he gets claustrophobia writing in the same room. The new stimuli also give him a broader perspective. There are times when I can't move from my home desk for weeks. I feel so nestled, so snug-like-a-bug. Other times, I can't move around enough—like when I travel: I feel so free, so unencumbered. I am always motivated to write in airplanes; the sense of movement becomes a catalyst for ideas to run free. The same thing happens when I'm near a beach. I'm inspired by the sound of the waves.

If travel is not on your radar at the moment and you can't find the time or the place in your home, rent a room. There are more and more commercial places popping up that provide office space by the hour or by the week for writers. In fact, most of these facilities provide wireless access, in case you need to do some research on the Web or read or respond to e-mails.

The Process

Let's say you've made the commitment to write: you're getting up every morning, turning off the phone, the TV. You've placed a Baroque CD in your CD player, music ideal for stimulating the creative juices. You've cleaned off your desk, placed a candle or flowers by your computer . . . Even then, the process of writing may not flow as easily as you'd like. The issues that come up are the same issues that arise in meditation or in any other spiritual or creative practice. You get to look at your insecurity, your inquisitiveness, and your restless mind.

Regardless of what comes up, keep your mind focused and your hand moving. Sit there until the time is up. Just like in meditation— whatever comes up while you're meditating, you maintain your posture until the chime or bell goes off. When you find your mind drifting away from its focus, you don't whip it unmercifully back into line. You gently shift it back to its focus. In writing it's the same way.

However, when the time is up or when it's clear you need a break, put down your pen or set your computer to sleep and get up, stretch, take a walk, go to a movie, change the scenery. When you've had enough distance, come back, reread what you've written, and then write some more.

There will be times where you will need to get away from the writing altogether, sometimes for days or weeks. It's okay. Trust those instincts. Write something else. Read other people's writing. If you take the necessary distance, when you do return, you'll be more detached. Those words that need to be added or eliminated, fine-tuned or rephrased, will jump out at you. And you'll see your writing in a whole new light.

Once there is a comfort level with the words you have written, try reading them out loud to friends or family members. Read to people you can trust, and who will offer you honest feedback. Since we are our own best critics, you may want to read your words into a tape recorder and play them back a few times. I do this when I want to hear the rhythm of a chapter or if I need to know the exact timing of a presentation.

When you feel confident with your work, try out your skills by writing an article, a newsletter, or a book on something that genuinely interests you.

ARTICLES

Writing an article or a series of articles is an ideal vehicle to articulate your message and attract your audience. Think about submitting an article to an online magazine, an e-zine. Search the Internet for websites that are looking for content and that attract the same audience you do, or a wider audience than you currently reach. Since the Internet allows for limitless input and limitless users, you could write and write and never run out of venues.

Walk around your local bookstore and pick out the magazines that you are drawn to and would like to see your article published in. Copy down the editor's name and the website of each publication. When you get home, look up the website and see what topics they are looking for, write your article, and submit it. There will usually be submission guidelines, the length and topics they are looking for in an article. Be sure to follow their instructions. The editorial readers have little time to deal with submissions that don't write to the needs of their publication and their audience.

Write a short article for your local newspaper or a magazine. Begin with a short article and gradually work up to a longer one. Once your article is published, you may even find yourself considered an expert. Who knows, they may love your article so much, they may ask you to propose a column. Your column may get picked up for syndication. After all, how do you think syndicated columnists get started?

Rick Levine started out writing a daily horoscope column for one website, Beliefnet.com. From that one single exposure, Rick's column was picked up for distribution by Visionary Network, the company that publishes Tarot.com and I Ching.com on the Web. His column has become so popular, it is now published by AOL, MySpace, Google home page, Third Age.com, and Netscape.

Rick says, "Writing a periodical column, whether it's daily, weekly or monthly, is like doing yoga. In other words, it's a practice you continue doing and it develops as a process of its own. It's about showing up and writing. Writing a column is also one of the best forms of advertising. My business has tripled from the exposure." [2]

In fact, while you're writing articles, consider that they could become chapters for your book or content for a newsletter. I have been able to use a number of my articles to help promote upcoming workshops, consultations, and other books. These articles have helped me to spread the spiritual/holistic marketing gospel, and my audience has grown considerably from the broader readership.

NEWSLETTERS

Writing a hard-copy or online newsletter every month or every quarter keeps your audience abreast with what is happening in your business. A newsletter helps you define your business while your audience is kept up-to-date with new information that will support their growth.

James Strohecker, president and cofounder of Health World On-Line, says: "For the last ten years our e-newsletter, *Healthy Update*, has provided a dynamic link to our subscribers. By providing the latest news, expert information, and resources in the world of alternative medicine and wellness, they can use the newsletter to improve the quality of their everyday lives. The newsletter has been a vehicle to maintaining a meaningful relationship with our subscribers. On a practical basis, we have received our best client leads for our programs and services." [3]

Dr. Mark Albion, founder of Making a Life, began writing his newsletter in March 1996. His mission was to communicate with service-minded MBAs, by inviting them to participate in surveys on what they considered the value in business. The survey became so popular that Dr. Albion was invited to deliver an official address to the United Nations in June 1996. That summer, he began to write real-life stories about altruism in business, and the newsletter quickly grew from a readership of 2,300 to reaching thousands of readers in eighty-seven countries.

Because the newsletter is more time-consuming to write, it's now available by paid subscription. His readers seem to have no qualms about paying.

"Each month," Dr. Albion says, "I try to engage, inspire and challenge people to find ways to make a living by what they get, and make a life by what they give. In each newsletter I ask my readers to reflect on one central life question, such as 'Are you a consumer, or a citizen?' or 'Why do you work so hard?'— questions that encourage them to bring humanistic values and civic responsibility into their life's work. My global mission is a world of peace where business is used to uplift the human spirit and alleviate poverty and suffering on our planet . . . and for every business to appreciate that one's spirit is as important as one's intellect, and that purposeful work leads to profitable work." [4]

You may have noticed in your e-mail inbox how many people use their newsletter to "sell" their services. I would not recommend doing this, unless you send out a calendar of upcoming events that your audience looks forward to receiving. Offer your audience pertinent information that will educate them regarding new trends, ways to stay healthy, save time, or save money. A thinly veiled vehicle for marketing your product or service will not be sustainable. In fact, it could turn prospective clients off. When your content provides value, your network will expand exponentially.

YOUR BOOK

Now, you don't have to write a book, although Dan Poynter, author of *The Self-Publishing Manual* and eighty other books, suggests that you do. "Everyone has a book inside them," he tells us, "and no one should die before writing one. So, as long as you are still alive, why not write one?" [5]

The question is, what do you want to write? What story is burning inside you to become known? Is it fiction? Nonfiction? Whatever the story is, be sure that you are passionate about it, because you may be spending the next few years writing it.

The trick is to not become overwhelmed by the prospect. Start by writing down some thoughts you have about the direction of the book, the topics you want to cover, which could become chapter headings. Then, pick one of the topics you feel most inclined to write about and start writing. Follow your heart.

Jerry DiPego, a dear friend and the screenwriter for *Phenomenon, Instinct, Message in a Bottle,* and *The Forgotten,* and author of *Cheevey, Keeper of the City,* and *Forest Things,* shares why he writes:

> I'm very stimulated by a story that the universe sends me—even the beginning, and the ghostly outlines of a story. As my excitement quickly moves into the sharing of this idea, that's the motivation. Once I feel the workings of the story, and my emotional responses to it, and the promise that it can mean something, say something, I want to shout, *Hey, gather around and listen to this.* But of course I have to write it first. And this challenge is stimulating, too, because it's when I write a story that I truly discover it. And then, full of the true discovery of the tale, I want to honor it by writing at my best, I want to make it sing, I want to come as close as I can to the story that's running in my head and heart. So it's the honoring of what's been given to me that stimulates me, and I take courage from that and try to do justice to what has captured me and driven me to put it on the page. [6]

Writing in Brahmā

Writing anything, particularly a book, because of its length, shows us how easily we move in and out of the three stages of creativity—the three faces of Brahmā, Vishnu, and Shiva we looked at in Chapter Four.

First, there is the Brahmā stage, visioning what the book is about. Meditating on what words and thoughts we might want to surface, allowing those thoughts to germinate in the crevices of our being, wandering through the thought waves of the mind. We don't have to know everything about the topic; we only have to know that it's something we ourselves want to explore. And even when the idea surfaces, it's always about going deeper, envisioning the different directions you can go in, to describe an aspect you or your audience never thought about before. This is what the Brahmā stage is all about. So, honor this time. Don't rush it. And know that you will be returning to it again and again.

Writing in Vishnu

Clearly, your book will never get written if all you do is think about it. So, at some point, we must move into Vishnu, the worker, the accomplisher. We must discipline ourselves to sit, breathe in the information that we have received from Brahmā, and breathe out into Vishnu. The cycle of Vishnu starts when we begin to type our thoughts into the computer or write them out freehand.

Keep writing; don't edit yet. Wait until all the words and thoughts are on the paper, wait until all the energy and excitement has dissipated, and your brain feels like it's been turned inside out—and then pause. Move away from your work; don't try to draw blood from a stone. Take a walk! Go to a museum, meditate, read someone else's book that inspires you. You may be sitting, watching a movie, when one line might trigger you to rewrite a sentence, or a paragraph, or add a whole new chapter. You never know where an idea will come from. When you start to really listen to everything and everyone around you, your writing will deepen, and come alive.

For this reason, I don't believe in writer's block. I think if we allow ourselves the necessary pause, listen to what our inner voice is telling us to do or where it's telling us to go, we will return to our book, eager and excited to forge on. Ultimately, our work is a process of layering ideas.

WRITING IN SHIVA

The Shiva stage is part of this pause, this letting go. Once we let go, we can "let come" the new thoughts and ideas. We can welcome them, think them through, and know when it's time to move back into Brahmā, visioning, or when it's time to move into Vishnu, writing down the thoughts, and gracefully move back into Shiva, letting them go again. The Shiva stage lets us know when it's time to distance ourselves, when it's time to give the writing away to an editor or to a friend for their feedback. The more we open ourselves to others' critiques and support, the better the writer we become. Shiva shows us when the book is done; it's a state that lets us stay detached from the feedback and at the same time listen sincerely to our readers' response.

By moving in and out of these stages, we honor the writing process, we honor the magnificence of our innate gifts. When we listen to the voice that tells us what stage we are in and when it's time to move into another, we can trust that we will be guided.

THE PERKS OF WRITING

There is so much for us to gain from writing. We gain entrée into and become a channel for our wisdom to surface. Our access to language increases; we become more articulate with our message. And if the writing is worthy of praise, we will receive the recognition and acceptance we deserve.

If Suze Orman hadn't written her first book, *The Laws of Money, the Lessons of Life*, who would have known about her? Do you think she would be on Home Shopping Network or have her own radio or TV talk show, now viewed by millions of people? What about Deepak Chopra, Tony Robbins, Wayne Dyer, Stephen King, Carolyn Myss, Joyce Carol Oates, or John Gray? Do I need to go on?

There are huge incentives to writing books, newsletters, articles, and columns. Doors fling open with opportunities you may never have conceived of. No longer will you find yourself hiding out, confined to your little home office or bedroom typing away in complete solitude. If your writing is favorably received, there will be journalists ringing your cell phone, radio and TV hosts banging down your door inviting you to appear on their shows, conference coordinators calling you, begging you to speak on their panel or present a keynote address.

Can you imagine the thrill of seeing your book sitting on a bookshelf in a bookstore? Having a bookstore call you for the third, fifth, or tenth time to say, "Please send another sixty books. We can't keep your book in the store"? "When are you coming out this way? We want to introduce you to our audience." How delicious is that?

When you start hearing from strangers who e-mail you and say, "Thank you so much for writing that article. It totally changed my life!" all the effort, time, sweat, joy, and sacrifice you made to write the article or the book to communicate your message will not have been in vain. In fact, the satisfaction you get may propel you to write even more.

As spiritual marketers, we write to share our knowledge, to inform people about our service or product, to let others know how and why our business is uniquely applicable. When our audience reads what we have written, they either connect with our information or not, resonate with our words or not. If we don't express our thoughts, how will our audience know about us, or, more importantly, know what we know? And why it might matter?

An Epiphany

While touring in Mexico not too long ago, I had an epiphany. I realized that every four to five years, I write a book, and then I move. I cannot move before the book is complete, because I am birthing and there is the need to nest. But when the book is finished and I'm ready to print it or send it off to be reviewed or published, then I can move.

The move becomes a physical manifestation of the growth I've experienced from the writing. I am a different person. As I sculpt the words, the paragraphs and chapters, I remold myself. As I weed out the excessive statements, the run-on sentences, the nonsequential or inconsequential thoughts, I chisel away needless aspects of myself.

In this respect, I do attempt perfection. I don't always make it; and at times, I'm way off. But what the hell! 'Tis a noble goal to strive for!

When we dive into the music no one else hears, explore those subterranean crannies in our minds, and keep digging, we bring those jewels and gems to the surface. The more we drop into that place where we learn what is already known, the more we sharpen the spirit, discipline the mind, and honor the knowledge that has been given to us. When we develop the courage to explore the limitations of our minds and let go, when we respect what has captured our attention, and do justice to what has driven us to write and to place those precious words on that pearly white page, we become the author to our own future. This too is a noble goal to strive for!

For Further Contemplation

1. Do you enjoy the writing process? If you do, what do you love about it?

2. Are you uncomfortable with the writing process? If you are, what do you dislike about it?

3. Are you making excuses? If so, what are they? And do you know why you are making them?

4. Are you creating the quiet space for your thoughts to run free? Are you honoring the three stages of creativity while you write? As you build the writing muscle, are you finding joy in the process?

5. Have you started to write any articles? If not, think about some topics that might be of interest to your audience. Better yet, think about some topics that might be of interest to *you*.

6. Have you written a newsletter that could give added value to your customers and clients? Have people commented on it? If so, what are they saying?

7. Have you started to write your book? If not, what are you waiting for?

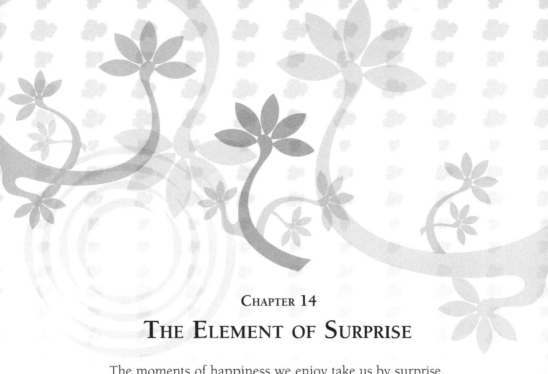

The Element of Surprise

The moments of happiness we enjoy take us by surprise.
It is not that we seize them, but that they seize us.

— Ashley Montagu, British anthropologist

Imagine walking into your office and finding a bouquet of flowers sitting on your desk. You open the card, and it's a thank-you note from a client you helped steer through an impending obstacle. Wouldn't that make your day?

A friend of yours purchases a new building for his business and you send him the gift of a consultation with a feng-shui practitioner to work with him on the colors and placement of his new furniture. You think that might bring a smile to his face?

When we add the element of surprise to our lives, we bring out the creativity, the fun, and the inventiveness within us. We elevate those with whom we share our delightful surprises—and brighten up both their day and ours. Unfortunately, many of us are so busy with our packed schedules that we have forgotten the pleasure we receive from *the surprise*.

I wonder. Has our society become so dense that the quality of the surprise is gone? Or is it temporarily on hiatus? Have we become so overstimulated and bogged down with the daily details that we don't think about gifting? Perhaps we've forgotten to touch base with our gentle hearts, forfeiting those tender moments of appreciation. Perhaps the act of kindness is now taken for granted. Maybe it's a sign that our current state of affairs has become so left-brained, so hyper-rationalized, that we need to be reminded to use other parts of our brain to become more intuitive and creative.

As spiritual marketers, we have many avenues by which we can reclaim our awareness of and access to the surprise. We can think about the people we work with, our coworkers and clients, and by what means we can uplift their day. We can call a colleague and share a funny joke. We can surprise a client by treating them to theater tickets or a basket of fruit, bringing them a fresh idea or a new contact.

Look at Oprah, for heaven's sake! She surprises her guests every day—with books, clothes, food, CDs, cars. She introduces long-lost twins who have never met, provides housing and schools to families in Africa, and is always present during a crisis to give whatever is needed. Is it any wonder, beyond her warm-hearted personality and smarts, why she has one of the highest-rated talk shows in TV history?

Look closely at the people you know who have great relationships. You may notice that they are always raising the bar, for themselves and for each other. They read new books, explore new restaurants; they go on interesting or exotic vacations. They're always growing, challenging themselves and creating intrigue. They never stay stagnant.

According to Edith Soto, an Aura-Soma practitioner whose work gets us in touch with our innate awareness through color, Magenta is the color that corresponds with the quality of surprise.

"The color magenta correlates with the eighth chakra," she said, "the center above the crown of the head, which is associated with divine love. Magenta represents the element of surprise and *the loving of little things*. It's not what we do, but how we do it. . . . We can set a table and throw the silverware in a pile and scatter the dishes and napkins around for people to fetch on their own: or we can light candles, play soft music, place flowers on the table, and use crystal napkin holders next to each plate."[1]

Magenta, a complex color, brings together the spirituality of violet, the passion of red, and the intense love quality of pink. Magenta is identified with the element of surprise because it's not just about presenting the surprise, it's the timing, the right gift, and knowing that the person receiving the gift will enjoy it.

SURPRISED ANYONE LATELY?

When was the last time you surprised someone? I am not talking about the shock of scare tactics, the kind of negative surprise that has made horror films the largest-grossing genre, nor am I referring to the obligatory "surprise" of someone popping out of a cake at a birthday party. I mean that gesture that tickles the heart and brings a smile to someone's face. For that matter, when was the last time you surprised *yourself*?

The stories that follow are about people who took the initiative and became inventive in their gifting. By doing so, they transformed themselves or someone else's workday, stimulated a rapport that was getting stale, or solved a problem in a way that evoked discussion, promoted a shift or fruitful action, and created monumental results.

A Surprise Vacation

Sally was recently divorced, very unhappy with her job, and her mother had just passed away. She was very depressed and knew there was a big shift about to happen in her life, but she didn't know when or how it would manifest.

One morning, she was sitting in meditation, when all of a sudden a little voice inside her told her to go to Italy. She had no clue where this thought came from. She didn't know anyone who lived there. But she'd always dreamed about Italy. So Sally decided to take a little vacation, and visit this country of her dreams.

On the third day there, sitting in a coffee shop, she met Kenneth, a man she had known from high school. He too was on vacation alone. He had come to Italy to explore the possibility of opening a restaurant there. He had family in Italy. Long story short, Sally and Kenneth are now happily married and living in Italy. They opened a café where Sally is experimenting with her favorite pie recipes and Kenneth is making Italian pasta dishes.

This unexpected vacation totally transformed Sally's life.

Surprised by a Stranger

Just when we think we're all alone in the universe, a stranger reaches out for no other reason than to express pure, unadulterated compassion.

I lost my shoe getting off the train in New York City. It literally slipped off my foot from the ledge of the platform and fell under the train. I was so embarrassed, so upset by my lack of composure; I stood there perplexed and helpless.

A woman passing by, who had seen the incident, walked over to me and without hesitation opened a bag containing a new pair of shoes and gave them to me to wear until I got home. The shoes were my exact size, a nine narrow. A coincidence? I was blown away by the fact that the shoes fit, and in awe of her generosity.

We exchanged cards. As soon as I returned home, I sent the shoes back to her and included a gift certificate for two to a lovely restaurant. She was so thrilled to receive this gift—which, to my mind, was very small compared to the gift she had given me—that she called me and asked if I would join her at the restaurant. I did, and we have been friends ever since. Only later did I recall that in ancient times, the highest form of respect was shown by touching the feet. I felt extremely honored.

DELIGHT YOUR CUSTOMERS

We can always surprise our customers by giving them something we know they will appreciate. A vitamin company that I order supplements from brought this kind of gifting to my attention. Every other month, I order vitamins from this company and every once in a while they send me an additional bottle of supplements, at no additional charge. I never know when they are sending them, but I'm always grateful when the gift comes. It gives a boost to my day and shows me that this company is thankful for my business and appreciates my continued support.

Think about the ways you can surprise your customers and let them know they are valued.

SHOW COMPASSION

Salespeople in general are focused on the bottom line. They will oftentimes go out of their way to make sure they get the highest commissions. They'll rush through the process of working with one customer, to get to another who may provide a larger profit. But how often do salespeople demonstrate empathy? Here is a case where a salesman did.

Connie needed a new bed, urgently. Her back was killing her from a recent fall, she was visiting a chiropractor every three days, and she hadn't slept in two weeks. Her current bed was over ten years old and too soft. She needed a new one, fast. When she went to the furniture store to order a new bed, she mentioned her situation to the salesman. He immediately called the manager and asked that her bed be delivered the next day instead of with the usual one-week delivery time.

Connie was in shock. She had never experienced this kind of service before. The salesman didn't do much. He simply made an additional call. But for Connie, his call made the difference of being in pain for one more day rather than for another full week.

Now, where do you think Connie will go the next time she needs a bed? Where do you think she will send her friends when they need a new mattress?

It doesn't take much to shift gears and discover ways in which we can be of service to others, make their lives easier rather than making sure our needs or, in this case, our commissions are covered first.

Surprise the Boss

There are so many ways we can say thank you to our boss or to the people we work with. We don't have to wait until their birthday or Christmas to show them our appreciation. When we notice someone having a hard day, we can think about how we can bring the element of surprise into his or her workday, and transform it.

Susan was having a challenging week at her advertising agency. Her mother was ill, her son was in trouble with the police, and her car had to go in for service. She was stressed out, to say the least, and not very pleasant to be around.

Unbeknownst to Susan, her secretary, Ruth, called a reflexologist, a practitioner who specializes in foot massage and who happened to work in the same building. Ruth gifted her boss with a much-needed treatment. Susan, now totally relaxed, was extremely grateful for this gift. And you can bet that Ruth and the other employees enjoyed having their boss return to a balanced state.

GET YOUR CLIENT'S ATTENTION

I love this story, because it transformed my understanding of the "conversation piece." While attending college, I had a part-time job working at Mister Marvin's, a small high-end women's boutique in Southfield, Michigan. Every season, Marvin, the owner, would purchase one or two designer outfits that he knew his clients would not be able to afford.

One day, Marvin placed a very expensive Rudi Gernreich pants outfit on the wall. The women who shopped there were shocked to see the price tag on this outfit and asked me, "Why is Marvin carrying such expensive clothes? They're priced for movie stars."

When I buttonholed Marvin and asked him why he did this, his reply was, "I always have at least one expensive item in the store. I know the price is beyond my clients' budgets, but you must admit, it adds to the allure of their shopping experience. It has stimulated conversation, yes? That's why I do it."

GIFTING CAN GET OUR PRODUCT
THE ATTENTION IT DESERVES

Jack was a client of mine some years ago. He owned a company that manufactured specialty knives. Jack's knife was unique because it was rust resistant and perfect for boating, fishing, and camping trips. He tried to contact a whole range of TV and magazine editors to promote the knife, but no one responded.

I suggested he send one of his knives as a gift to the editor of every boating, yachting, fishing, and camping magazine he wanted to be affiliated with. Jack followed my advice and when the editors received their gift, they were blown away. They were impressed not only by the quality of the knife and all its uses, but because Jack had gone out of his way to send the knife, and was generous and without expectation. In response to Jack's surprise, ninety percent of the editors wrote articles about Jack's knife, which resulted in over one million dollars in sales his first year.

Add Humor to Your Workshops

For those consultants who offer workshops or introductory programs, be aware that these courses can get pretty mundane unless we approach them with a sense of humor. When we bring humor and the element of surprise into our class, our audience is grateful for the reprieve.

Midway through a workshop, Michael, a well-known seminar leader, walked into the room wearing a clown outfit. He said nothing about his baggy clothes, his big red nose, or his huge black shoes. He just kept talking about the subject at hand.

The audience was in stitches. Later that day, when everyone came back from lunch, there were balloons all over the room. Michael was no longer wearing his clown outfit. He was blowing bubbles. He later explained that he used the clown outfit, the balloons and the bubbles as a metaphor for how we were to incorporate the new information he was disseminating—lightly, and with a sense of humor.

Be Unique in Your Pricing

Eduardo, a businessman living in Mexico City, is involved in corporate mergers around the world. His job is to find companies that need investors, and connect them with businesses that want to invest in reputable enterprises. These investments can yield millions of dollars in revenue. What is unique about Eduardo is that he offers something that most people in his line of work never do: Eduardo does not charge a retainer fee for his services. He only makes a percentage if the agreement goes through.

When Eduardo explained this to a Russian company that was looking for investors and a Canadian company that was interested in making an investment, both companies were so thrilled that there would be no up-front cost that they signed the agreement papers right away. After the deal went through and both partners were pleased with the results, the Russian company not only gave Eduardo an additional bonus of $10,000, the same amount he would have made had he charged a retainer fee, but told two other companies about Eduardo's services—and word continues to spread. We can always find ways to build our business and have it be based on trust.

BE COURAGEOUS

I would like to cite my son as an example here, because he is one of my best teachers. Brian presented me with a huge surprise the first time I listened to his CD, *Pranam*. I was quite familiar with the poetry of Rumi, Issa, and Lao Tzu, the poet-saints of the Sufi and Taoist traditions whose works Brian had drawn on for his compositions. But the surprise came when I heard the music that accompanied the poetry. These were not your obligatory melodic sounds. You know, the droning or airy unmemorable music you hear while doing hatha-yoga stretches, or the elevator tunes you hear as background to conversations in restaurants. The words were captivating, of course, as they originated from these great poets, but the melodies were incredibly dramatic and riveting.

His music stopped me in my tracks, and forced me to give it my total attention. For the first time, I understood how these poets had affected Brian musically. I began to appreciate my son's passion, his musical genius, in a whole new light. It takes great courage to trust one's intuition, one's musical sensibilities, one's heart, to go against the norm. A true positive deviant, Brian reflects such raw honesty through his music that to this day, I remain astonished by what comes out of him.

Lighten Up Your Conference

A workshop presenter I know was looking for a unique way to open his conference and decided to surprise the participants by doing something he'd never done before. This was the story he shared with me:

He walked into the workshop wearing a Balinese sarong, and sauntered to the center of the room. Two bare-chested colleagues accompanied him. The first carried a ceremonial drum, which he struck in staccato rhythms. The second carried a bundle of six-foot-long ropes slung over his shoulder.

The presenter then requested each of the participants, who numbered about one hundred and formed a circle around him, to select a partner. He asked the partners to decide which of them wanted to be "the dog," and which one wanted to be "the master."

The "masters" were instructed to take a rope, so that they could leash their "dog" and go for a walk. "Dogs" were instructed to remove their shirts, shoes, and socks, walk on all fours, and only speak to other dogs. Masters were encouraged to talk with as many other dog owners as they could in an allotted time period. It was suggested that dogs exhibit a high degree of curiosity in sniffing and pawing their fellow canines. The masters were asked to discuss with other masters the reasons why they were attending the conference.

The net result of this exercise was to dramatically transform what had begun as an anxious and reserved group of men into a playful, curious, and spontaneously interactive group, and to reframe their thinking by reducing their "self-talk" filters.

It was notable that many of the "dogs" bonded so well with one another that they maintained a close, active dialogue throughout the remainder of the four-day conference. Likewise, the "masters" continued extended conversations with their fellow pet owners. I do believe the workshop presenter accomplished his goal.

Bring Magenta into Your Gifting

I used to rarely wrap presents, and when I did, it was not done with much love or attention. Wrapping seemed like such a waste of time. Why bother, I thought. The receiver was just going to open the package and throw the paper and ribbon away anyway.

And then I attended a friend's birthday party. There were about sixty people invited to the celebration. It was in my friend's beautiful home and I had volunteered to show people where the bedroom was so they could place their coats on the guest bed. As each person walked in holding their potluck dish and birthday present, I noticed what people had brought and how each present was wrapped so beautifully, how each dish looked like it could be sold at Whole Foods. It was fascinating to see. One person walked in bearing a beautiful box wrapped in purple and pink iridescent paper and a lavender pink bow. Another person had a peacock feather peeking out from the giftwrap. There were elaborate soufflés and homemade casseroles and fruit baskets overflowing with exotic fruit.

And then there were people who brought cartons of deli food or what looked like leftovers. As I watched each person offer their gift and their plate of food, there seemed to be a quality of refinement among those who had taken the time and care in wrapping their presents and preparing their dishes. They seemed to hold themselves differently from those who had clearly thrown something together or purchased something at the last minute. It wasn't subtle; it was all too apparent.

It triggered my conversation with Aura-Soma expert Edith Soto and made very real to me how she described the meaning of the color magenta—that it wasn't the gift itself, but the love and care that went into the selection. The conversation brought back the memory of another story.

An old woman from India was very poor, but she wanted to bring her beloved teacher a present. The woman searched her garden for days until she found the perfect tomato. She approached the teacher bearing the tomato with so much love and tenderness that when the teacher received it, he cried. He later spoke about this woman's gift and how he felt receiving the tomato. He said, "It is never about the gift, but the feeling with which it is given."

I now take the time to wrap my gifts. Most importantly, this one act, I've noticed, can spill over into other parts of our lives. Taking the time, not rushing through tasks just to get them done, brings reverence into our lives. It is a direct reflection of our consideration and respect for those we are gifting, and of how we value ourselves.

THE TRUTH IS

We don't have to wear magenta to be in the spirit of gifting or to experience its reverential quality. We don't have to wait until there is a crisis, a birthday, or a holiday to be generous. This element, this manifestation of surprise can be an ongoing, stimulating adventure that continues to promote optimism, stir a change of heart, and cultivate an ever-expanding spiral of openness and potentiality.

By making the first move, not waiting for someone to gift us first, we celebrate those we care for, begin to trust in the power of our imagination and lightheartedness, and see firsthand that the return on our investment, whether tangible or intangible, will always be beyond price.

For Further Contemplation

1. When was the last time you surprised someone you work with, with words of gratitude?

2. When was the last time you surprised yourself by doing something totally spontaneous?

3. Have you witnessed someone going through a hard time? What did you do to support them? How did you let them know you were concerned?

4. Have you surprised your clients lately? If not, what could you do that would totally thrill and inspire them?

5. How can you add the element of surprise to your presentations?

6. Do you own any clothing that has the color magenta in it? If so, have you worn it lately? If not, would you consider purchasing something that has this color in it? You may be very surprised by the feeling it produces just by wearing it.

7. What could you do right now, today, to express humor, celebration, or delight?

CHAPTER 15

DISCIPLINE

It is better to conquer yourself than to win a thousand battles.
Then the victory is yours. It cannot be taken from you,
not by angels or by demons, heaven or hell.

— Gautama Buddha

What goes through your mind when you hear the word *discipline*? Do you cringe? Tighten your stomach muscles? Squeeze your brows? Close off from the possibility of hearing the word in a way that might be beneficial? Or even joyful?

If you've experienced these reactions, you are not alone. One of the first translations for *discipline* in the dictionary is "punishment," with "training by obedience" close on its heels. So is it any surprise that those of us who grew up in Western culture and experienced parental, teacher, or vocational "discipline" have these negative responses, and think of discipline as a kind of chastisement?

In the East, discipline is viewed as a sign of spiritual maturity, a divine practice. The feeling of friction that arises when we apply discipline is acknowledged as a churning of the ego, a refining of the intellect, and a noble act.[1]

Discipline, at its most essential level, comes from the Latin word *discipulus*, "student," "disciple"—someone thirsty to learn. Discipline, above all, means *awareness*: action in alignment with the experience of being *awake*.

In chapter six of the *Bhagavad Gita*, an ancient scripture of India, we listen in as Lord Krishna instructs his student Arjuna to attain a state of balance and equanimity in the midst of a ferocious battle. The chapter entitled "The Yoga of *Atma Samyama*," "the yoga of self-control," informs us through Krishna's conversation with Arjuna how we can perform our *dharma*, our right action, and how to act on the Battlefield of Life with consciousness and integrity. Instructing Arjuna, Lord Krishna is determined to dissolve Arjuna's ignorance and arm him with the right understanding.

Arjuna responds to Lord Krishna by saying, "O Lord, these signs of saintliness are not found in me. Moreover, if I were judged by such a standard, I would undoubtedly fall short of it."[2]

Like Arjuna, we don't think we are up to the task of exhibiting these qualities. We think we have to be saints in order to achieve self-control in our lives. The truth is, a disciplined life is not about punishing ourselves for indulging in a whim every now and then, nor is it about rendering ourselves incapable of enjoying life's pleasures. Accomplishing authentic happiness, abundance, and satisfaction requires a certain measure of self-control—that is, a conscious commitment to a clear and worthy goal, and to a course of action that will take us there. Without it, transformation cannot occur.

There is a story about Tiger Woods, the beloved saint of golfdom and one of the most highly respected athletes of our era. Tiger, as we know, is no stranger to discipline. Since a child, he has been a dedicated student under the tutelage of his father.

The story goes like this: Tiger was encouraged by his coach to modify his golf swing to achieve a higher level of expertise and precision. Tiger knew that in order to keep playing and winning, his swing would have to change to adjust itself to his evolving and maturing body. Each time he made the decision to adjust his swing, his game suffered; but only initially. Once his body became acclimated, comfortable with the new movement, his game was transformed; he excelled above and beyond all spectators' expectations, as well as his own.

This account validates Tiger's exceptional disciplined nature and his willingness to "lose" in order to win. The sacrifices he made at each step, as he went on to play the game for higher and higher stakes, enabled him in the long run to become a stronger player.

SACRIFICE

Sacrifice. Another word loaded with subliminal innuendo, especially when we hear phrases like "I sacrificed everything to make you happy." "Do you know what I sacrificed to buy you that house?" Throughout the ages, victims of sacrifice have ranged from prisoners to infants to vestal virgins, who suffered such fates as burning, beheading, or being buried alive. No wonder we wince when we hear the word.

The truth is, we make sacrifices all the time. They are a good thing! They determine our preferences, our priorities. Conscious business owners sacrifice spending money in one place to spend it more wisely in another. Conscious consumers sacrifice driving clumsy, gas-guzzling SUVs in order to reduce car emissions and protect the environment—well, maybe not such a sacrifice after all. I'd bet that as a youth, Tiger Woods made the sacrifice on several occasions to practice his swing instead of playing with his friends.

But what does the word actually mean? *Sacrifice* literally signifies "to make sacred": to offer something of value, to give something away, willingly, to something or someone we value more highly. It takes discipline to be clear about what we value, to recognize what is sacred, what is worth holding fast to, and what is worth letting go.

DISCIPLINING OUR CRAVINGS

We come into this world with all kinds of cravings. We desire a flourishing business, wealth, a beautiful office, a lovely home. We want meaningful relationships, the freedom to take vacations, buy beautiful clothes. Pursuing these cravings can bring us a certain amount of enjoyment and satisfaction. Longing for them can even become the catalyst for us to be more productive and creative, the spark that ignites the "fire in the belly."

But what about those unrealistic cravings, like renting an office or a house we can't afford, advertising without the budget to back it up? In other words, living above and beyond our means? We accumulate tons of stuff we know we don't need, but we purchase it anyway. These cravings can appear harmless, until we find ourselves in debt. That's when we so easily slide down that slippery slope and lose ourselves, our money, our loved ones, our clients and our jobs, all in the pursuit of these cravings.

And then there are those insidious cravings, the ones that creep up on us when we're not looking. Like when we're having a wonderful time going about our day, and all of a sudden, WHAM! We suddenly find ourselves out of control and powerless because we have forgotten to be moderate in how we use our senses—we eat too much, drink too much, talk too much.

And because we have forgotten to remain true to our innate awareness, we fall. We may not fall far or hard. We may not lose our way for long. But we find these indulgences have repercussions. And they can take days, months, even years to repair, when they can be repaired at all.

The Repercussions of Our Actions

As business owners, now based in spiritual/holistic principles, we walk a fine line as we try to stay authentic, uncompromising in our integrity, and still yield to the ebb and flow of the moving target we are striving for: success. We want our businesses to prosper, to reach a critical mass, to become so popular that we reach the tipping point and experience more than our fifteen minutes of fame. But this is where we walk that tightrope that can lead us across to the other side of the circus arena—or where we slip and fall, from the *lack* of discipline.

And if you think the decisions you make are challenging now, as you climb the ladder toward that burning vision of victory, wait until you get close to the top. It only gets hotter! The more success you attract, the more significant your actions become. The higher you climb, the more your behavior is observed under the microscope of public scrutiny. Haven't you seen it all too glaringly in the media?

You may recall what happened to one actor when he slid under the media's microscope. Remember Hugh Grant's rendezvous with a prostitute? Mr. Grant's little tryst ended up in headlines around the world and the late-night talk shows had a field day. What about when Martha Stewart was found guilty of obstructing justice and lying to investigators about her well-timed stock sale? Personally I adore Hugh Grant's acting and I think Martha is quite the businesswoman. And, as we all know, even bad publicity can generate . . . publicity. But how do our actions affect the mainstream, the culture, our families and those around us? What are the messages we are sending out to the universe when we indulge in these activities?

Remember Howard Dean's famous "shout" during the 2004 primary? Although it was documented that he was shouting along with his supporters, a directional mike had stripped off the roar of the crowd, leaving Dean's shout the only sound audible on tape. The media had not captured the true picture. In less than one minute, news spread around the world that Dean was unstable. This intentional or unintentional faux pas by the media, and Dean's momentary emotional indulgence, cost him his chance at the presidency.

One doesn't have to think long or hard to recall other episodes where politicians, celebrities, or even people that we know, slipped, due to lack of discipline.

I am not implying that we should walk timidly through life in mortal fear of making mistakes. We're always going to compose our little splashes in the world. The point is: whether the "splash" we create has a positive impact or a negative impact, we will be remembered by that splash! And there will be repercussions.

There are two areas in our lives where discipline, conscious action, is especially vital. They are a bit subtler, more insidious than the sexual, business, or political slips we've just looked at. The two areas are *speech* and *food*.

Food is a topic that I don't believe has ever been discussed in a business manual or marketing book, at least none that I'm aware of. And yet food is one of the most significant underlying factors influencing every physical, mental, and emotional action we perform.

And speech. Why speech? Because our speech can determine the outcome of any personal or professional relationship; and because it is one of the most essential frameworks for perfecting our spiritual marketing chops.

DISCIPLINING OUR SPEECH

Do you ever think about how your words will fall on the person listening to them? Every word we say can change a person's state. Our words can make someone smile, or make them weep. Words can uplift someone's day, or inhibit them for years.

One man told me it took him decades to get over one comment his art teacher in elementary school had made in front of the class. The teacher had called the students one by one to the front of the room to grade their art assignments. When she asked my friend to come to the front, he stood tall and proud. He was so happy with his project. After all, he had stayed up all night working on it. Her comment to him and to the class was, "You call this art?"

Those words haunted this young boy for years. Not until he was in his forties, five therapists later, did he trust his artistic instincts again and start painting. He now sells his art worldwide.

I'm sure you've been in this position, or something like it: You've hung up the phone after a call from a client who was very annoyed. The shipment that was meant to arrive for their big event got stuck in a snowstorm in Denver. It's no one's fault. Still, your client was extremely upset, and now so are you. You're shaky and irritable. You hang up the phone and another client calls with a problem. No doubt: your sweet and compassionate nature will not spontaneously arise. In the aftermath of the previous call, you start barking at this woman. The emotional domino effect has been triggered, and you're on a roll. Then, you apologize for your behavior. That is, if you're even aware that your response was inappropriate and uncalled-for.

Or how many times have you reacted to someone's sarcastic remark with a sarcastic remark of your own, only to realize afterwards that you were better off not saying anything? Too often, we let our tongues speak before our minds have a chance to catch up or catch on. We are in regret. We're agitated and feel off balance for the rest of the day.

THE FOUR GATEKEEPERS OF SPEECH

Is it true? Is it kind? Is it beneficial? Is it the right time?

These questions were introduced during a talk I attended by Gurumayi Chidvilasananda, meditation master and spiritual head of the Siddha Yoga lineage.[3] The instant I heard these words, I knew they were going to change the way I communicated. As soon as I returned home from the talk, I typed the words on a sheet of paper and placed them by my telephone.

In speaking about these questions, Gurumayi called them "the Four Gatekeepers of Speech." Usually, when we think of a gatekeeper, we think of a guard who prevents us from entering a place. But, when I began to ponder these questions before I spoke, they saved me from making silly mistakes, and reacting from a knee-jerk place. In fact, the gatekeepers became an open door—allowing me entrance into a quality of spaciousness, thoughtfulness, and ease.

Years later these words still remain in a prominent place by my phone and I ask them of myself in every conversation with clients, friends, and family. These questions define the attributes of appropriate speech. They bear repeating and contemplating: Is it true? Is it kind? Is it beneficial? Is it the right time?

SILENCE

Remaining silent, taking time to pause before we speak, is another powerful discipline. Silence is golden. When we practice silence consciously, it adds strength to our speech and renews our energy to work and play and enjoy our lives more fully.

Tom, a successful real-estate agent, maintains silence every Sunday. He told me that the reason he practices this discipline is twofold. First, he gets to rest his voice. And second, when he resumes speaking, his words have more potency, more resonance. He said there is a distinct quality, a richer vibration in his words, especially at the start of his workweek. His clients have noticed a difference in how he speaks to them, his associates have made references to his powerful presentation skills, and his relationship with his family has become sweeter. In fact, the whole family has decided to maintain silence on Sunday along with him.

Not only do we receive greater clarity about ourselves; when we maintain silence, we become more receptive to and have greater insight regarding other people's intentions and needs. And in the world of marketing and communication, this heightened sensitivity stands us in very good stead.

Here again, meditation can be our greatest ally. Meditating before starting our day can tune us in to our thoughts and speech before we even utter a word. When we meditate, we are less apt to say things we don't mean, or express emotions that are out of character.

Food

What comes out of our mouth ultimately has an intimate relationship with what goes into our mouth. This may be hard to digest (pun intended), but choosing our words becomes easier when we have eaten the appropriate foods.

It has taken me years to truly comprehend the role food plays in our lives. Its repercussions are beyond comprehension. Haven't you noticed how you feel when you eat certain foods? Some foods stimulate us to get up and dance, while others make us feel so heavy, all we want to do is curl up on a couch and go to sleep. What happens when we eat too much? Too little? Every morsel of food we put into our bodies has an effect on how we act, think, and feel. I'm sure you've heard the phrase, "You are what you eat." It's true! David Wolf, an authority on nutrition and author of *Naked Chocolate* and *Eating for Beauty*, says,

> "You are what you eat" is an eternal and inevitable law of nature. It is the ultimate verdict of quantum physics. We consist of mostly an energy field with atoms very distantly placed. If those atoms come from the food, air, and water we ingest and, when ingested if those atoms are treated

with greed, neglect, and lack of spiritual consciousness, our atoms and energy fields cannot function at the highest level. If those atoms and energy fields are treated with love and lots of it, there is no telling what we can achieve.[4]

When you think about it, is there anything—other than the air we breathe, and the thoughts we think—that determines our state of mind more than food? Food affects our entire nervous system. And depending on the quantity and the quality of the food, our physical and emotional reaction will be one of either chaos or coherence.

CHAOS AND COHERENCE

Gabriel Cousens, author of *Conscious Eating* and *Spiritual Nutrition: Six Foundations for Spiritual Life*, uses the phrase *chaos and coherence* in referring to the body as a field. Conditional on what food we place in our field, he says, "we will reap either chaos or coherency."[5]

Coherency is what we experience when we are watchful of the food we eat, when we want to feel energetic and clearheaded. Chaos is what we reap when we overeat, and feel sluggish and vague.

The reality of this contrast became quite evident once while I was presenting a workshop. I hadn't eaten a proper breakfast—I think I popped a few cherries into my mouth, because I was late. By the time lunch came around, I was starving. During the meal, I ate way more than I needed because I was so hungry. I also included a huge chocolate-chip cookie for dessert, thinking that the sugar would give me the extra boost I needed. Of course I knew better, but I was already in a mentally chaotic mode. In delusion and denial, thinking I could get away with it, I didn't. I was so exhausted from the rise and fall of my glucose level, I could hardly stand for the duration of the course.

Self-sabotage

Why do we eat foods we know are not good for us? I believe it is a form of self-sabotage. Many of us are masters at achieving this unconscious, sinister behavior. Each of us can think of examples: We have a big appointment and instead of taking care of ourselves by getting a good night's sleep, eating properly, and exercising, we fill our minds with doubts. We begin to think we aren't good enough, smart enough. Before we've even met anyone at the appointment, we've created the sabotage, mentally. And these thoughts have led us to those foods that numb us. You know what those foods are for you.

I used to be a master at numbing myself. Any emotional upset would lead me right to a piece of chocolate cake. The sugar would immediately make me dizzy, my mind would get fuzzy, and it wouldn't be long before I'd experience a full-blown migraine. When I ate bread, all I wanted to do was sleep. And if I ate after seven at night, I'd be up all night digesting my meal. It's a tightrope! No question.

And what about those of us who consistently eat more than we need? Perhaps we are hungry for something else. Here is where we need to ask ourselves some probing questions. Where do these cravings come from? What is at their origin? Are we not trying to fill a void that may otherwise be satisfied with love, affection, mutual sharing, the delight of creativity, or the simple joy of being alive? Are we not consuming things to make up for something else that we may be missing? What *would* make our life fuller, richer, and bring us more joy?

Really think about these questions. If we don't drown out the answers with more food, we make room for the voice to surface. Then we can listen and take positive action. By distinguishing the real hunger from the hole we're trying to fill, we end the self-sabotage. We end the chaos. We are at the top of our game—the game of business, the game of love, and the game of life—through the exercise of our own awareness.

Reining In the Senses

Look, I'm no saint. I certainly have not mastered the art of discipline, although lately I have been focusing my energies toward that end. I have crashed and burned more than a few times when I didn't curb my enthusiasm or pause to think before jumping into a situation I soon regretted. There have been times when I've spoken prematurely and had to apologize for my behavior. Unleashed anger has propelled me into plenty of feuds. Whatever our addictions or obsessions may be, the process required in lassoing the senses, homing in on those reins, never ends.

Living intentionally, communicating honestly, eating and enjoying life with discipline is a minute-by-minute, day-by-day, conscious effort to *be* better, *feel* better, *live* a happier, more productive, love-filled life. Our lives and our businesses suffer when our actions are not disciplined. The pendulum swings from one extreme to the other. These subtle and insidious slips cut into our freedom, carve stumbling blocks into our mental pathways, and without notice pull us down into the depths of unconscious behavior. We lose sight of our goals, and our life comes to a screeching halt.

So, how can we master our senses? How can we transform our ordinary perception into an extraordinary vision and make the most of this initiation? We can stay alert. We can notice when our lives are working and when they are not. We can stay mindful of our true needs and the needs of others. And when these needs are not being met, we can pause, refresh our resolution, reshape our journey, and then . . . keep moving.

For some of us, it is mastering our intake of food; for others it is disciplining our speech. For most of us it is seeing discipline as a joyful, enriching experience that has monumental rewards.

The rewards are not just something that we get *from* discipline, but something rewarding in the experience of discipline itself: something exhilarating, something spacious, something balancing, something that breathes.

THE INVITATION TO EMBARK

There is a fierce, tumultuous roar
in the background of your consciousness.

>Do you hear it?
>Are you listening?
>What is the roar asking of you?
>Where is it beckoning you to go?
>Who is it beckoning you to become?
>What story have you been attached to,
>>that you are now asked to let go of?

It's time to make bold moves; have you noticed?

>Fear no longer can be your motivation—
>only the courage to evolve.
>Listen closely.
>What is it that you have yearned for?
>How many times has it showed its face
>and you've looked the other way,
>>laughed it off, or been too timid to proceed?

Now that you have been initiated into the Science of Spiritual
Marketing, are you ready to listen to the throb of you own heart and
allow the wildflowers to push through?

Perhaps these words by Rumi will propel you:

>The prophets have wondered to themselves, "How *long*
>should we keep pounding
>
>this cold iron? How long do we have to whisper into an
>empty cage?" Every motion
>
>of created beings comes from the creator. The first soul
>pushes, and your second

soul responds, beginning, so don't stay timid. Load the ship and set out. No one knows

for certain whether the vessel will sink or reach the harbor. Cautious people say, "I'll

do nothing, until I can be sure." Merchants know better. If you do nothing, you lose.

Don't be one of those merchants who won't risk the ocean! This is much more important

than losing or making money. This is your connection to God! You must set fire to have

light. Trust means you're ready to risk what you currently have. Think of your fear and

hope about your livelihood. They make you go to work diligently every day. Now

consider what the prophets have done. Abraham wore fire for an anklet. Moses spoke

to the sea. David molded iron. Solomon rode the wind. Work in the invisible world

at least as hard as you do in the visible. Be companions with the prophets even though

no one will know that you are, not even the helpers of the *quth*, the *abduls*. You

can't imagine what *profit* will come! When one of those generous ones invites you

into his fire, go quickly! Don't say, "But will it burn me? Will it hurt?" [1]

And please accept my blessing for you . . .

May the exciting, rapturous, loving, abundant life
you always sought to be a part of, be yours.

May you be blessed with the wealth of liberation
and the wealth of the world.

May you hold on to the vision of your dreams,
and may your passion for your life and your work
be rekindled every day.

Respectfully,
Andrea Adler

THANK-YOUS

I would like to thank the following magnificent human beings who have demonstrated, above and beyond the call of duty, their love, support, and genuine concern for the birth of this book:

Brian Adler, my beloved son, who constantly reminds me of the gift of motherhood, and the necessity for structure and tension and release in my writing. He has been my inspiration and my anchor since the day he was born. And besides . . . nobody makes a room *swing* like he does. And no one plays the high hat so sweetly.

Cynthia Briggs, my trusted and benevolent editor, whose insight and intellect always makes me go deeper. She always hears my voice and the authenticity that wants to come through. Her thoughtfulness, depth of understanding, and generosity continue to astound me.

Indrani Weber, for her keen awareness of the truth and of what it takes to keep one's feet on the path, and her profound ability to impart that mindfulness. Thank you for waking me up.

Gene Mateson, who listened to chapters day after day, week after week, with rapt attention. Gene is my rock on the planet and is indispensable to my happiness.

Molly Duncan, of Desert Elements, for her imaginative, elegant cover design. For her patience, and for her generosity in allowing the use of her design throughout the book.

Denton Lesslie, for his graceful typesetting and book design, for his tenacity and desire for perfection, and for being the easiest, fastest person I've ever had the pleasure to work with.

Larry Dossey, whose critique helped me to fill in a significant piece—the inclusion of a more explicit global perspective.

To the following souls who were there when I needed them to read and listen, and offer their ears to this book:

Parvati Markus, Marty Rosenberg, Leland Lehrman, Bindu Hennings, Betsy Robinson, Ann Cafferty, Gayle Olander, Kenneth Guard, Jeff Elster, Ana Benscoter, Edith Soto, Peggy Dugas, Joyce Libutti, Janet Davidson, Linda Mertz, and Art Miller.

And to the Siddhas, my teachers:

Bhagawan Nityananda,
Baba Muktananda,
and Gurumayi Chidvilasananda,

who endlessly teach me how to listen.

Suggested Reading

Personal Development

The Four Agreements, Don Miguel Ruiz
The Six Pillars of Self-Esteem, Nathaniel Branden
Taking Responsibility, Nathaniel Branden
The Artist's Way: A spiritual path to Higher Creativity,
    Julia Cameron
Emotional Alchemy, Tara Bennett-Goleman
Remembering Wholeness, Carol Tuttle
Nonviolent Communication: A Language of Compassion,
    Marshall Rosenberg
*Ask and It Is Given: Learning to Manifest Your Desires (The
    Teachings of Abraham)*, Esther and Jerry Hicks

The Spiritual Path

The Yoga of Discipline, Swami Chidvilasananda
Where Fear Falls Away: The Story of a Sudden Awakening,
    Jan Frazier
The Power of Now, Eckhart Tolle
Enthusiasm, Swami Chidvilasananda
The Biology of Transcendence, Joseph Chilton Pearce
Illuminata: A Return to Prayer, Marianne Williamson
Peace Is Every Step, Thich Nhat Hanh
The Mandala of Being, Dr. Richard Moss

CAREER AND CONSCIOUS LIVING

Holding the Center, Richard Strozzi Heckler

The Tipping Point: How Little Things Can Make a Big Difference,
Malcolm Gladwell

The Anatomy of Buzz, Leonard Rosen

Mind Maps at Work, Tony Buzan

Attracting Perfect Customers: The Power of Strategic Synchronicity,
Stacey Hall and Jan Brogniez

Megatrends 2010: The Rise of Conscious Capitalism,
Patricia Aburdene

Giving: How Each of Us Can Change the World, Bill Clinton

MEDITATION

The Heart of Meditation: Pathways to a Deeper Experience,
Swami Durgananda

Zen Mind, Beginner's Mind, Shunryu Suzuki

I Am That: The Science of Hamsa from the Vijnana Bhairava,
Swami Muktananda

Notes and Permissions

The Journey of Initiation

1. Excerpt from *The Soul of Rumi*, translation by Coleman Barks. New York: Harper Collins, 2002.

Chapter 1, The Root Chakra of PR

1. Stuart Ewen, http://www.bway.net/~drstu/chapter.html, from *PR! A Social History of Spin*. New York: Basic Books, a division of Harper Collins, 1996.
2. Ibid.

Chapter 2, Connecting to Source

1. SYDA Foundation, personal communication, May 2007; used by permission.
2. Pema Chödrön describes shenpa in her audiobook *Getting Unstuck: Breaking Your Habitual Patterns and Encountering Naked Reality*. Boston: Shambhala, 2004.
3. Michael Slater, personal communication, June 2005; used by permission.
4. Steve Palevich, personal communication, June 2007; used by permission.
5. Patricia Aburdene, *Megatrends* 2010: *The Rise of Conscious Capitalism*. Charlottesville, VA: Hampton Roads, 2007.

Chapter 4, The Three Stages of Creativity

1. Cynthia Whitcomb, personal communication, July 2005; used by permission.

2. Trimurti image: http://www.gurjari.net/ico/Mystica/html/trimurti.htm.

3. Brahmá image: http://www.gurjari.net/ico/Mystica/html/brahma.htm.

4. Vishnu image: http://archaicgifts.com/display_item. php?item=ATB-101&refer=google_adwords&kw=vishnu; http:// www.gurjari.net/ico/Mystica/html/vishnu.htm.

5. Shiva image: http://images.google.com/imgres?imgurl=http:// www.aloha.net/~ruth/shiva09-333.jpg&imgrefurl=http://www. aloha.net/~ruth/&h=400&w=333&sz=21&tbnid=EiYg_j0mJdUp KM:&tbnh=124&tbnw=103&prev=/images%3Fq%3Dshiva%26u m%3D1&start=1&ei=xkK_RpySH43ahQPikp3TCw&sig2=uCZ4s YPbst0IpI81OD8sgA&sa=X&oi=images&ct=image&cd=1.; http:// www.gurjari.net/ico/Mystica/html/shiva.htm.

6. Nataraj image: http://www.lotussculpture.com/nataraj1.htm; http://en.wikipedia.org/wiki/Nataraja.

Chapter 5, Moving Beyond Our Comfort Zones

1. Alexandra Katehakis, personal communication, June 2006; used by permission.

2. CNN correspondent Peter Bergen: I was struck by this comment when I read it and wrote it down. I've since been unable to locate the original source.

3. The Dalai Lama on compassion: http://hhdl.dharmakara.net/hhdl speech.html.

4. Marshall Thurber on positive deviance: personal communication, April 2006; used by permission.

5. Lane Houk on Herocare: personal communication, May 2006; used by permission.

6. *Oprah*, George Clooney interview: I've been unable to trace the date of this specific show segment.

CHAPTER 6, THE POWER OF OUR STORY

1. The Pet Rock: http://www.virtualpet.com/vp/farm/petrock/petrock. htm.

2. The Greyston Foundation: *Instructions to the Cook: A Zen Master's Lessons on Living a Life That Matters*, Bernard Glassman and Rick Fields. New York: Crown Publishing, 1997.

3. Salem: Salem Chamber of Commerce, 265 Essex Street, Salem, Massachusetts 01970, (978) 744-0004; used by permission.

4. Just Coffee, www.justcoffee.org, February 2005; used by permission.

5. Ibid.

6. Jay Jurisich of Igor International: personal communication, September 2006; used by permission.

7. Brandhome: http://www.brandchannel.com/features_effect. asp?pf_id=274, a brand consultancy specializing in brand development and extension in Asia. Doris Ho, principal consultant, August 2005; used by permission.

CHAPTER 7, RITUAL AND CEREMONY

1. YouTube: Deepak Chopra, interview with journalist Judy Martin, http://www.youtube.com/watch?v=NnETVXKkvNU&mode=relate d&search=.

2. Bruce Coldham, personal communication, July 2007; used by permission.

3. Dr. Richard Moss, personal communication, July 2007; used by permission.

Chapter 8, Mind Mapping

1. Tony Buzan, http://www.buzanworld.com/mindmaps/.

Chapter 9, Our Soulful Collateral

1. Carolyn Myss, *Personal Healing* (audiobook). Louisville, CO: Sounds True, Inc., 2003.

2. Claire Papin, personal communication, June, 2007; used by permission.

3. Jesse Dillon, personal communication, June 2007; used by permission.

4. Gary DeRodriguez, personal communication, June 2007; used by permission.

Chapter 10, Building Bridges

1. The National Academic Press, http://www.nap.edu/books/0309 100267/html/.

2. For books on network science, see http://www.amazon.com/s/ref= nb_ss_b/002-9854451-2830461?initialSearch=1&url=search- alias%3Dstripbooks&field-keywords=Network+Science&Go. x=0&Go.y=0&Go=Go.

3. Albert-Laszlo Barabasi, *Linked: The New Science of Network*, http:// www.andreas.com/faq-barabasi.html. New York: Basic Books, 2002.

4. For a discussion of six degrees of separation, see Wikipedia, http://en.wikipedia.org/wiki/Six_degrees_of_separation.

5. For a discussion of the small-world phenomenon, see: http://en. wikipedia.org/wiki/Small_world_phenomenon

6. Mark Granovetter: http://en.wikipedia.org/wiki/Mark_Granovetter.

7. The William Jefferson Clinton Foundation: http://en.wikipedia.org/wiki/Clinton_Foundation.

8. *Larry King Live*, encore performance, October 2, 2005.

Chapter 11, Leveraging Our Assets

1. Jade Luna, personal communication, February 2007; used by permission.

2. Gilbert Pichinich, personal communication, February 2007; used by permission.

3. Eiko Okura, personal communication, March 2007; used by permission.

4. Ibid.

Chapter 12, Responding from Abundance

1. Raphael Kellman, *Matrix Healing: Discover Your Greatest Potential Through the Power of Kabbalah*. New York: Harmony, 2004.

2. White Dog Café: http://www.whitedog.com/. Judy Wicks, personal communication, April 2006; used by permission.

3. Victor Heredia, personal communication, May 2006; used by permission.

4. Kay Snow Davis, personal communication, May 2006; used by permission.

5. Spryte Loriano, personal communication, June 2007; used by permission.

CHAPTER 13, WRITE TO LEARN

1. Julia Cameron, *The Artist's Way: A Spiritual Path to Higher Creativity*. New York: G. P. Putnam and Sons, 1992.

2. Rick Levine, personal communication, May 2007; used by permission.

3. James Strohecker, personal communication, June 2007; used by permission.

4. Mark Albion, personal communication, July 2007; used by permission.

6. Dan Poynter, personal communication, June 2003; used by permission.

7. Jerry DiPego, personal communication, March 2006; used by permission.

CHAPTER 14, THE ELEMENT OF SURPRISE

1. Edith Soto, personal communication, March 2007; used by permission.

CHAPTER 15, DISCIPLINE

1. Gurumayi Chidvilasanda, *The Yoga of Discipline*. South Fallsburg, NY: SYDA Foundation, 1996, pp. 42, 44, 49.

2. *Bhagavad Gita* 6:139–40, 142–43, as quoted by Gurumayi Chivilasanda in *The Yoga of Discipline*, p. 6.

3. Personal communication; used by permission of SYDA Foundation. See also Gurumayi Chidvilasanda, *The Yoga of Discipline*.

4. David Woolf, personal communication, May 2007; used by permission.

5. I borrow the terms *chaos* and *coherence* from Gabriel Cousens, *Spiritual Nutrition: Six Foundations for Spiritual Life and the Awakening of Kundalini*. Berkeley, CA: North Atlantic Books, 2005; used by permission.

INVITATION TO EMBARK

1. Coleman Barks, "Work in the Invisible," *The Soul of Rumi*, pp. 19–20. New York: Harper Collins, 2002. Used by permission.

ABOUT THE AUTHOR

Andrea Adler is the founder of Holistic PR, an international speaker, workshop presenter, and the author of three books on spiritual/holistic marketing. Andrea specializes in supporting entrepreneurs, small and large business owners, and students on the relevance of spirituality in the workplace. She teaches a practical philosophy of consciousness that demonstrates how to integrate spiritual practice and psychological self-inquiry into a concrete and fundamental transformation of people's lives and their businesses. Andrea lives in Santa Fe, New Mexico.

For a calendar of upcoming workshops and presentations by the author, and for further information on CDs, books, consultations, and other material, please visit:

www.HolisticPR.com

505-983-7777

andrea@HolisticPR.com

- Keynote presentations
- Workshops
- Corporate and individual consultations
- Corporate trainings
- Tele-classes
- Books and CDs
- Becoming a Certified Holistic PR Consultant